Salmon and Science

Salmon and Science

*A short history of our knowledge
of Atlantic salmon*

DEREK MILLS

COCH-Y-BONDDU BOOKS
2016

Two hundred and fifty copies of
Salmon and Science
have been printed in the
Coch-y-Bonddu Books Angling Monographs Series
This copy is number ....
In addition there are twenty-six hardbound copies

© Coch-y-Bonddu Books Ltd 2016
Text © Derek Mills
ISBN 978 1 904784 73 9
Coch-y-Bonddu Books Ltd
Machynlleth, Powys, SY20 8DG
01654 702837
www.anglebooks.com

Dedicated to
my family

Contents

Preface

Although the life history of the Atlantic salmon is now well-known, and the similar life histories of the six species of Pacific salmon are also well documented, more detailed information on the salmon is less accessible. This is not surprising as the work undertaken on the salmon, usually by government or university scientists, is extensive and most of the results of such scientific enquiry are published in government publications or in the scientific literature. What scientific literature, you may well ask, and where can it be found? Over the years there have been a number of scientific journals in which these results appear, most of which can be consulted in public libraries that, even if they don't have them on their shelves, will arrange to obtain them on a temporary basis. Local universities might also allow one to read them in their library. Government publications are usually to be found in public libraries.

Some of the most popular journals that include fisheries literature are: *Fisheries Research; Journal of Fish Biology; Fisheries Management and Ecology; Aquaculture and Fisheries Management; ICES Journal of Marine Science,* and *Canadian Journal of Fisheries and Aquatic Science.*

Other publications appear periodically and the most useful are the proceedings of Atlantic Salmon Symposia produced by publishers such as Blackwells and Fishing News Books. There are a limited number of these printed, usually only a few more than the number of delegates present. Amazon occasionally have some, but at a price.

For some time the Atlantic Salmon Trust produced what popularly became known as Blue Books. They covered many aspects of Atlantic salmon ecology and are sometimes available from the Atlantic Salmon Trust. Proceedings of the Annual Meeting of the North Atlantic Salmon Conservation Organisation (NASCO) are also a useful reference to on-going salmon research.

A considerable number of books on the Atlantic salmon have been written, many of them beautifully illustrated in colour, and these are referred to in the text. All are worth consulting.

This is not meant to be a detailed treatise on the science of the Atlantic salmon and is not a textbook; indeed such a volume would be of immense size reaching proportions to vie with the *Encyclopaedia Britannica*. This work is simply to provide the reader with a sense of how an understanding of the life and ecology of the salmon has developed over the years. It is set out as a review describing the highlights in the course of these observations, and how these have advanced our knowledge and helped the direction of future work.

The current literature on salmon investigations, including the results of ongoing or recently completed research, is immense and much of it is only available in very expensive books. These works are referred to in the bibliography but for close scrutiny it will mean either a visit to an appropriate library or an expensive outlay. I briefly refer to the papers presented at salmon symposia to give the reader a flavour of salmon topics of importance at the time of publication, and of the general interest being shown by delegates to these.

I do not cover the commercial salmon fisheries but must point you in the direction of an excellent comprehensive work on the subject entitled *The Salmon Fishers* by Iain Robertson and published by the Medlar Press in 2013.

Only passing reference is made to books specifically about rod-fishing for salmon: this has its own voluminous literature.

Derek Mills
Melrose, 2016

Acknowledgements

Over sixty years involved with salmon as a scientist, university teacher and angler I have met many people in all walks of life, many of whom have become my close friends. I am grateful to all of you for your advice and friendship.

In particular, my thanks go to colleagues and friends in all regions of the salmon world – Canada, the Faroes, France, Greenland, Iceland, Ireland, Norway, Spain, Sweden, the United Kingdom and the USA.

I should like to thank Paul Morgan for his encouragement at all stages in the book's production and Peter Mackenzie for all his work on its design and layout.

Many of the books cited, with the probable exception of some of the scientific works, are available through the second-hand book trade, either from specialists such as Coch-y-Bonddu Books, or through the usual internet searches.

CHAPTER ONE

Our Early Knowledge

Our basic knowledge of the life history of the Atlantic salmon (*Salmo salar*) extends back many years, indeed centuries. Judging by the Acts of the Scottish realm the salmon was protected at various stages of its life history as long ago as the times of David I (1124–1153) and William the Lion (1165–1214). At that time it was enacted that dam dykes should have a gap large enough in which to allow a three-year old swine, well fed, to stand, thus allowing free passage of salmon to their spawning grounds. The fact that the salmon was a migratory fish entering the rivers from the sea to spawn was therefore established. The Romans had long before then noticed the habit of salmon to leap at falls, hence their Latin name *salire* being the Latin word for 'to leap.' However, Willughby and Ray refer to the first description of the salmon in an old Latin folio as *Salmo omnium autorum*.

Hector Boece recorded the basic knowledge of salmon and their migrations in his treatise *Historia Scotorum* of 1527 (translated by George Buchanan in 1571). Their observations centred on the migration of the salmon and speculation regarding the juvenile stages. Peder Clausson Friis (1545–1614) surmised that salmon bred in fresh water, that the young fish spent a period in the river before migrating to sea, and that once there they grew rapidly and carried out extensive migrations. Further observations of the salmon, particularly behaviour of the adults, came much later. Probably Francis Bacon in his *History of Life and Death*, Izaak Walton in *The*

Compleat Angler and Michael Drayton in *Polyolbion* were among the first to record their observations on salmon behaviour. Walton refers to young salmon going to sea and it would seem that the stage to which he is referring is the smolt stage:

> It is said, that after he is got into the sea, he becomes from a samlet not so big as a gudgeon, to be a salmon, in as short a time as a gosling becomes to be a goose. Much of this has been observed by tying a ribbon, or some known thread, in the tails of some young salmon, which have been taken in weirs as they have swimmed towards the salt water, and then by taking a part of them again with the known mark at the same place at their return from the sea, which is usually about six months later.

It was to be some considerable time before the enigma of the status of the salmon parr that many scientists of the time considered to be a separate species, *Salmo salmulus,* was resolved. Willughby in 1686, Pennant in 1761, Sir Humphry Davy in 1832, Yarrell in 1836 and Parnell in 1840, all thought that the parr was a separate species from the salmon. However, the truth that the parr is really the young of the salmon was one of the oldest of all the theories. On the River Annan the fishermen universally entertained this idea: it had prevailed for at least a hundred years. In 1794 a Mr Hutchinson of Carlisle had observed that:

> If from the sides of a true salmon fry, or smolt, the silvery scales be carefully scraped, the young fish will show all the parr markings concealed by these scales.

In *Days and Nights of Salmon Fishing on the River Tweed,* first published in 1843, William Scrope drew attention to the fact that, in his opinion, the salmon parr was the juvenile stage of the salmon and it was only at the time of migration in the spring that the scales of the larger parr, that were destined to go to sea that spring, developed a silver deposit (guanin) on their scales thus concealing the river colouration so like that of a brown trout. His near neighbours on the Scottish Borders, Sir Walter Scott and James Hogg, the Ettrick

Nil fuit unquam

Sie impar sibi

Two salmon smolts with scales partially removed from the lower fish.
(*from* Scrope, Days and Nights of Salmon Fishing on the River Tweed).

Shepherd, were of the same opinion. Hogg had undertaken some experiments to confirm these observations, the results being published in the 'Maga' (*Blackwood's Magazine*). This conclusion did not satisfy others interested in this phenomenon. James Bertram in *Harvest of the Sea* (4th edition, 1885) refers to an amusing conversation between James Hogg and a friend:

Shepherd: *I maintain that the saumon comes aye back again frae the sea till spawn in its ain water.*

Friend: *Toots, toots, Jamie! Hoo can it manage till do that! Hoo in the name of wonder can a fish travelling up a turbid water frae the sea, know when it reaches the entrance to its birthplace, or that it has arrived at the tributary that was its cradle?*

Shepherd: *Man, the great wonder to me is no hoo the fish get back, but hoo they find their way to the sea first ava, seein' that they've never been there afore!*

Dr Knox in *Fish and Fishing in the Lone Glens of Scotland,* published in 1854, dwelt at length on this subject. His main contention centred around the presence of salmon parr where adult salmon were not thought to be present; the absence of eggs in female parr but well-developed roe present in male parr; the ability to fertilise eggs from adult salmon with milt from the roe of male parr; its dentition that resembles that of a trout more than that of an adult salmon; and the number of spines in the various fins. He refers to the various measurements of the fins of Tweed parr, and records his observations on the presence and subsequent absence of parr in some Tweed tributaries. He also refers to the observations of a Mr Young from Invershin who confirms Dr Knox's observations as being close to those of his own. A Mr Hannay, in writing to Dr Knox, remarked that he had assisted a Mr Gillom with his experiments with salmon parr ever since 1838 and "neither of us entertain the slightest doubt but that the parr becomes a salmon the third year after being spawned." He then goes on to describe their experiments by the River Dee in Aberdeenshire. The first of these experiments were conducted in 1835–6.

So, the subject of the parr being a juvenile salmon raged on. Many of the scientists over a long period of time considered the parr to be a variety of trout. Agassiz, Sir Humphry Davy, Sir William Jardine, Willughby and Yarrell had all considered it to be a separate species, *Salmo salmulus*. However, in the 1830's John Shaw and Andrew Young carried out salmon breeding experiments at Stormontfield Ponds near Scone Palace on the banks of the Tay and concluded that parr were the young of the salmon. The results of the experiments were summarised in *Blackwood's Magazine* (April 1840 and May 1843). The dispute, however, remained for some time and was documented by Henry Flowerdew in 1871 in a most interesting volume entitled *The Parr and Salmon Controversy*. It was reissued in 1883 under the title *The Parr, Salmon Whitling and Yellow Fin Controversy* in an expanded version to include a further debate involving the young of brown trout and sea-trout.

Evidence for the fact that the parr was one of the juvenile stages of the salmon (fry and smolt being the others) was demonstrated very convincingly in experiments undertaken by John Shaw that were published in the *Edinburgh Philosophical Journal* in 1836 and *The Transactions of the Royal Society of Edinburgh* in 1840. There are rare occasions when female parr do develop mature ova and Alan Youngson and David Hay in their beautifully illustrated book, *The Lives of Salmon,* published by Swan Hill in 1996, describe a sexually mature female from the Girnock Burn, a tributary of the Aberdeenshire Dee. The fish had produced 38 small eggs.

It had been previously recorded by Calderwood and Menzies that there was a significant downstream movement of parr in the autumn and it was thought that this heralded a second seaward migration at that time. This was discredited, as parr marked at that time did not return the following year but a year later.

However, even though the doubt as to whether the parr was a juvenile stage of the salmon or not had apparently been removed, anglers on the Tweed still continued to fish for parr and smolts and in the 1980's there were still anglers on the Tweed that were convinced that the parr was a separate species!

It is rather surprising to learn that a salmonid terminology was not produced for scientists until 1975 in a publication produced by the International Council for the Exploration of the Sea.

However, the knowledge of the basic life-cycle of the salmon was, by the late nineteenth century, generally accepted. There is no doubt that the young salmon-rearing experiments of William Brown at Stormontfield on the Tay from 1853 to 1861, involving the marking of smolts ready to go to sea, provided all the evidence needed to convince all but the doubting that salmon parr were indeed the young of salmon. Brown published the work in 1862 under the title *The Natural History of Salmon.* This work gives interesting information on the rearing of the young fish and the results of the recovery of those fish that had been marked and released. The smolts were marked in a number of ways; some by making a hole in the gill cover (operculum), others had a silver ring or copper wire inserted into the fleshy part of the tail or in the back by the dorsal fin, while some had the adipose fin removed or one lobe of the tail fin excised. The best recoveries as returning adult fish were from those that had the adipose fin removed. This fin never regenerates while the lobes of the tail fin do. Very few of those that had the ring attached were recovered.

Brown makes a number of interesting observations during the course of his investigations:

> In descending the river to the sea, smoults congregate in shoals, rise greedily to the fly, and become an easy prey to the angler. They proceed slowly, unless a heavy spate occurs at the time, which soon sweeps them into the ocean. The marked pond-bred smoults have been traced all the way from that place to the salt water – a distance of at least twenty miles.

The duration some of the 'smoults' remain in the sea was debatable and Brown's observations were soon going to be open to doubt when the results of the return of fish carrying numbered tags, attached by fishery authorities on the Tay and Tweed, were known. For example, it was shown from the release of 6500 smolts tagged with silver wire at Kinfauns on the River Tay in 1905 that the first returning adults came back more than a year later, all the recaptures being in the vicinity of the Tay. The fish returning after only one year at sea to spawn were termed grilse. Fish returning after two or more years were referred to as salmon.

A *Report of Investigations on the Life-History of the Salmon in Fresh Water* was produced by Dr Noel Paton in 1898 for the Fishery Board of Scotland: Salmon Fisheries series.

The tagging of smolts had been undertaken on the River Tweed some years earlier and in 1873 smolts were tagged at Heughshiel by the Experimental Committee of the River Tweed Commissioners. Calderwood gives a record in *The Life of the Salmon* of salmon-marking observations in Scotland prior to that of the Fishery Board in 1896. These records extend from 1823 to 1868 and include the marking of grilse, kelts and sea-trout. He also provides a detailed table of the River Tweed tagging experiments from 1851 to 1872.

It had been known for some years that the adult fish return to their own rivers to breed; as Ashworth in 1868 remarked that there

Tagging of Salmon on the Tweed at Heughshiel by the
Experimental Committee of the River Tweed
Commissioners. *The Daily Graphic* 6th Dec 1873

Tagging smolts at Heughshiel on the Tweed.

were distinguishing features in the shape of each class of fish known
to inhabit their different rivers. This observation was much later to be
open to some considerable doubt. When Dr Arthur Went visited a
salmon netting station at the mouth of one of the large salmon rivers
in southern Ireland he was told by the netsmen which particular
salmon was destined for which tributary. He then marked those fish
so that they could be identified later if recaptured upstream. Most of
the fish marked by Dr Went, when caught later, were not taken in
the tributary predicted by the netsmen, thus revealing the netsmen's
predictions were usually wrong. Dr Went gives an interesting account
of the salmon in Irish history in his Buckland Lectures for 1955
entitled *Irish Salmon and Salmon Fisheries.*

A breakthrough for further investigation into the salmon's life
came towards the end of the nineteenth century. It had been known
through work on carp and cod at that time that scale markings might
be interpreted as denoting the age of the fish in much the same way
as one can tell the age of a tree. The use of salmon scales as a means
of ascertaining the age and other biological conditions of the salmon
was almost certainly due to Mr HW Johnston who wrote an account

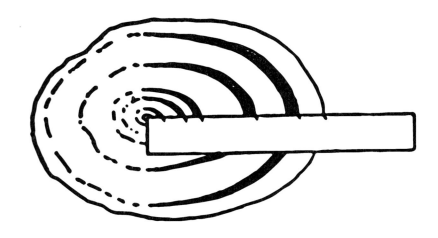

A diagram indicating the method of scale reading.

in the *23rd Annual Report for the Fishery Board for Scotland* in 1904 describing the technique. A popular article on the subject appeared in the *Dundee Advertiser* on 6th July, 1909. This was another step forward in our acquisition for more information on salmon from different rivers; the age at which they went to sea as smolts, the time they spent at sea, and if they had spawned more than once. All this could be learnt from the scales. While in the river the growth rings on the scales were spaced widely during the periods of greatest feeding during the summer and in the winter, when growth was minimal, the rings were close together, so, by counting the bands of closely spaced rings (denoting a winter) one could tell their age. Furthermore, not only can the age and history of the fish be read, but the length also at the end of any year can be calculated provided the length at capture is known. This possibility rests on the fact that the scale growth is proportionate to the increase in body length throughout the whole of its life. A projected image of the scale is measured from the centre to the edge of the scale and from the centre to the end of each winter band of the scale. Dr Jack Jones of Liverpool University gives a good description of estimating lengths from the scales of the salmon at the end of each year in the life of the fish in his monograph, *The Salmon,* published in the Collins New Naturalist series in 1959.

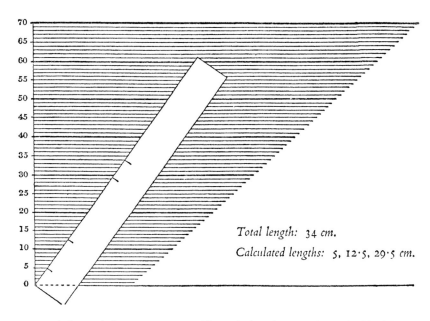

With the marked strip it is now possible to calculate the annual growth of the fish.

Such estimates depend of course on whether or not one knows the length of the fish at capture. It became standard practice to take scales from fish during most investigations, as it was then possible to know more precisely at what age the smolts were going to sea, at what age they were returning, whether they were coming back as grilse after one year at sea or a year or more later as salmon or multi-sea winter fish, and what proportion were returning to spawn a again. Many deductions could then be made from this information that could help managing the local salmon stocks.

As the salmon stops feeding on river entry it draws on its body tissues for nourishment, and this results in absorption of calcium from its scales resulting in scale erosion. When the fish starts feeding again on return to the sea calcium is once more laid down, but the erosion mark remains as a spawning mark. From the presence of this it is therefore possible to determine whether or not a fish has previously spawned. WL Calderwood described the spawning mark on salmon scales in a 1913 Fishery Board for Scotland publication.

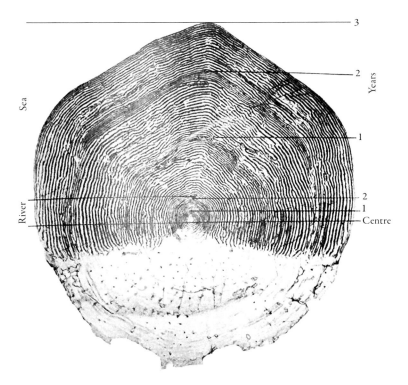

The salmon scale showing the annual rings or circuli.
(16½ lb, 35½ inch Spey salmon – 2 years as a parr in the river and then 3 years in the sea)

Calderwood provided more detailed knowledge of the growth of salmon from scale reading in his *The Life of Salmon*, 1908. PD Malloch from Perth had also been studying the scales of salmon from the Tay for many years, and described the results of his work on salmon scales in his excellent book, *Life History of the Salmon and Trout and Other Freshwater Fish,* published by A&C Black in 1910 and revised with many more illustrations of salmon scales in 1912. Both Calderwood and Malloch describe clearly the life-cycle of the salmon that has never been disputed.

The question as to whether or not adult salmon feed in fresh water on their return from sea was given some airing by Calderwood. He refers to the study of Hoek who examined 2000 salmon in the lower Rhine and found fish remains in only seven fish, while Ruesch

A female grilse bearing a silver wire tag at the anterior end of the dorsal fin. The fish was tagged as a smolt.

500 miles up the river at Basle examined 2162 salmon in four years and found food in only two male kelts. Occasionally mature male salmon have been recorded taking salmon parr and a student of mine found ripe male salmon parr in a mature cock salmon in a spawning tributary of the River Tweed. However, it is likely that this was simply an act of aggression against the parr that had intervened while the cock and hen fish were spawning.

With this newly acquired knowledge of salmon, along with information on the place and time of return of marked fish, investigations proceeded apace and information was gained on the age-structure of salmon returning to various rivers, in Scotland (by WL Calderwood, 1907, 1908 and Malloch, 1910, 1912), England and Wales (by JA Hutton, 1910), and Norway (by Knut Dahl, 1911). Malloch provided photographs of tagged adult salmon on their return to the river. Most of the tags shown are simply silver wire that has been threaded through the anterior base of the dorsal fin. The data on the recapture of many of these marked fish stimulated salmon biologists to extend their tagging experiments that led on to more detailed investigations that would improve our knowledge of salmon. This would be invaluable in helping conserve imperilled

23

salmon stocks on some rivers open to industrial development.

One timely observation made by Malloch and described in his book (1910) was the outbreak of a disease, the identity of which was never officially confirmed and cause never resolved. What was most important about these observations was that the same disease with the same identifiable symptoms, outbreak and spread in Scotland was to occur just over 50 years later. The disease first made its appearance in the River Eden near Carlisle, the following year it appeared in the Tweed, and the year following in the Tay. From then on it spread north to all rivers as far as the Thurso. It appeared chiefly in the spring, and then again in the autumn; both times of the year when the water is cold. It caused the deaths of thousands of fish covered in patches of fungus. Malloch refers to the study of this disease by J Hume Patterson of Glasgow who considered the disease to be *Bacillus salmonis pestis.*

Most salmon investigations undertaken in Scotland during the next twenty or more years centred on studies of scales collected during salmon netting on various Scottish rivers. These were undertaken by Calderwood, Menzies and Macfarlane and published by HMSO as official publications of the Fishery Board for Scotland. Some of the salmon rivers included the Aberdeenshire Dee, the Spey, Don, Forth, Tweed, Findhorn, Add and other rivers flowing into the Moray Firth and along the east coast of Sutherland.

Hutton also continued the work on salmon over this time in England and Wales, with much of it being centred on salmon from the River Wye (*Wye Salmon and Other Fish,* John Sherratt & Son, 1949). Menzies recorded the Scottish investigations in *The Salmon: Its Life Story* in 1925 and published by William Blackwood.

CHAPTER TWO

Increasing Our Knowledge

The large number of books published on the salmon during the 19th century was indicative of an increase in the attention being paid to this commercially important fish. It was therefore imperative that there was effective legislation to control its exploitation.

After some local Scottish salmon legislation in the early nineteenth century two important Scottish salmon fishery Acts were passed: the Salmon Fisheries (Scotland) Act of 1862 and the Salmon Fisheries Act of 1868. The first brought into being a small body of Commissioners whose duties were to fix the limits of fishery districts in Scotland; to fix a point on each river which would divide the upper from the lower proprietors; to determine the dates of the annual close time for each district; and to make general regulations as to the observance of the weekly close time, the meshes of nets, etc. Eighty-seven districts having been arranged, provision was made for the creation of District Fishery Boards. Very few of these Boards remained in existence for long.

By the Act of 1868 the powers and duties of District Boards were defined and extended. Each district was to have a superintendent and a staff of bailiffs.

In addition there was created the position of Inspector of Salmon Fisheries for Scotland, a government position coming under the control of the Scottish Home Department and later to be transferred to the Department of Agriculture and Fisheries for Scotland.

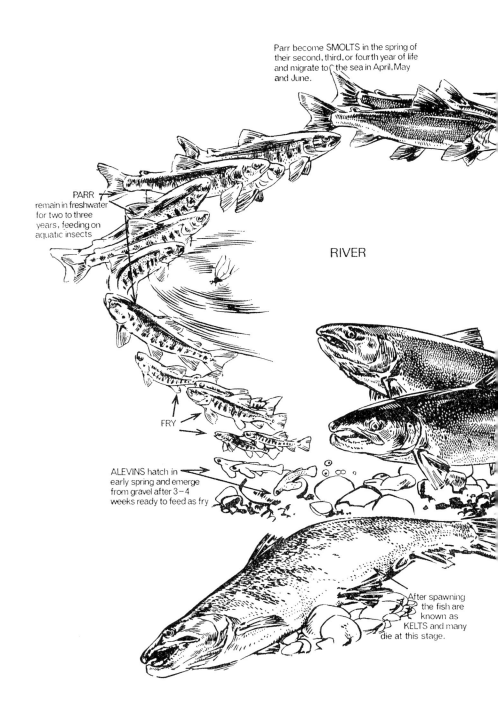

Parr become SMOLTS in the spring of their second, third, or fourth year of life and migrate to the sea in April, May and June.

PARR remain in freshwater for two to three years, feeding on aquatic insects

RIVER

FRY

ALEVINS hatch in early spring and emerge from gravel after 3 – 4 weeks ready to feed as fry

After spawning the fish are known as KELTS and many die at this stage.

Salmon travel long distances in the sea and feed on a number of marine organism such as sand eels, herring and plankton

SEA

On approaching freshwater the salmon stops feeding

EGGS are laid in gravel in late autumn

The life cycle of the salmon

Calderwood and Menzies held this position in turn, and undertook their salmon investigations in collaboration with the superintendents of the salmon district fishery boards.

Malloch, who was their contemporary, worked independently. Much of the work of Calderwood, Menzies and Malloch, summarised in the previous chapter, was to form the foundation on which later salmon investigations would be based. Frank Buckland should also be mentioned in this context; he, fifty or so years earlier in England, had held a similar position to that later held by Calderwood and Menzies in Scotland. His memory is honoured to this day through the Buckland Lectures that are held annually in various areas of the United Kingdom.

By the 1930's scientists at universities in the British Isles, Norway and Canada began to make a significant contribution to certain aspects of salmon biology. Government scientists were continuing their work in Scotland and achieving good results from the marking of smolts, adults and kelts and their subsequent recapture along the coast and on return to the river. Menzies in *The Salmon: Its Life Story* (1925) describes many of these results and suggests the likely areas frequented by the smolts while at sea. He also gives interesting accounts of the coastal movements of adult fish. For example, fish tagged on the Helmsdale were recaptured 125 miles south at Aberdeen, those marked on the Deveron were taken as far south as Cove, 120 miles south, and fish from the Spey were taken at Elie in the Firth of Forth, 150 miles to the south. Menzies points out that as most of the marked fish were caught to the south of where they were tagged and released, at least on the east coast. It appears from the results that salmon that have spawned approach their native river from the south when on their second journey to the river. Menzies also gave some thought to the likely destinations of adult fish while at sea and this proved to be of some significance as later tagging experiments proved.

Calderwood reviewed much of the current knowledge of salmon and described methods for the artificial hatching of the fish in *Salmon Hatching and Salmon Migrations*, the Buckland Lectures for 1930. In the eastern Canadian provinces of New Brunswick and

Nova Scotia AG Huntsman and HC White were experimenting on the return of salmon to two branches of the Apple River that flowed into the Bay of Fundy. The experiments included determining the time of return of fish that had been transplanted to the Apple as juveniles from their parent river, the Restigouche, that returned at a different time to the Apple fish. It was found that the introduced fish assumed the characteristics of the Apple fish and returned as adult fish at the same time as the native fish.

Later, Huntsman was to suggest that salmon entering the Bay of Fundy from neighbouring rivers would remain there throughout the whole period of sea feeding. His thoughts therefore seemed to run parallel to those of Calderwood who considered, from the results of his marking of adult fish at various Scottish sites that salmon from east coast Scottish rivers roamed over the whole of the North Sea. Calderwood was not surprised at the distance salmon travelled and quoted Knut Dahl from Norway who, in *Salmon and Sea Trout: A Handbook* (1918), refers to a fisherman returning from Newfoundland catching a salmon half-way between Newfoundland and Rockall, 1,000 miles from land in each direction. Calderwood was on the right lines when he remarked "We are able to picture the salmon ranging widely in the ocean in a way unsuspected by earlier observers."

In his Buckland Lectures Calderwood describes an interesting observation on the leaping behaviour of salmon. These observations were made at the Orrin Falls on the River Orrin, a tributary of the River Conon in Ross-shire. When Calderwood had the height of the falls measured it was 11 feet 4 inches. The height of these falls at normal river level is 12 feet. Only about one in every 15 to 20 fish were successful in their attempts to ascend. The fall is a sheer perpendicular one and the fish have to land in a slight hollow in the lip or crest to enable them to overcome the force of the glide over. Many years later Dr TA Stuart from the Freshwater Fisheries Laboratory in Pitlochry studied the leaping behaviour of salmon and his observations were recorded in a publication published in 1962 by the Department of Agriculture and Fisheries for Scotland in its

A salmon appears as though it will successfully ascend the Orrin Falls

Freshwater Fisheries Research series entitled *The leaping behaviour of salmon and trout at falls and obstructions*. The stimulus to leap is closely related to the presence of a standing wave, or hydraulic jump, and the location of the standing wave distant to the obstacle influences the success of the leap. Thus in shallow fall pools and pools below sloping weirs the standing wave is located too far downstream for the fish to strike the crest of the fall on the upward arc of its trajectory. If the fish strikes the falling water on the downward arc it is immediately swept downstream.

Pryce-Tannatt described a range of fish passes in connection with obstructions in salmon rivers in his Buckland Lectures for 1937. He was of the opinion that a sheer fall of 6 ft is probably about the maximum practicable for the great majority of salmon, even under the most favourable conditions, including plenty of room and depth below to enable the fish to develop the necessary velocity. He also considered the question of water temperature in relation to the salmon's ability to surmount obstacles. An obstacle that was difficult to ascend in winter at low water temperature would be surmounted with ease in the summer at warmer water temperatures.

This aspect was also covered by Calderwood in his Buckland Lectures, namely the question of temperature in relation to the ascent of the river by the salmon. He pointed out that the ascent of clean-run fish in winter is slow if the temperature is under 35° or 36° Fahrenheit. It is in the ascent of a main river and its tributaries that the effects of temperature are most apparent. When tributaries are colder than the main river, fish tend to remain in the main river until the temperature in the tributary reaches that of the main river. In *The Salmon Rivers of Scotland*, (Mills and Graesser), published by Cassell in 1981, Neil Graesser describes the effect of temperature on salmon ascending the River Cassley. The diagram (overleaf) depicting this movement is most revealing and shows that water temperature is inhibiting the upstream movement quite clearly. The salmon can enter the lower reaches of the river when the water temperature reaches 45°F but are unable to ascend the main falls until the water temperature reaches 52°F.

Prof. Hawkins and colleagues made estimations on the swimming speed of adult salmon. They found that upstream progress was initially quite fast – more than 10 km/day. Actual swimming speeds were considerably faster for short periods; even against quite high river flow rates speeds of more than 20km/day were quite common.

Hawkins found that fish started to move at dusk and Willie

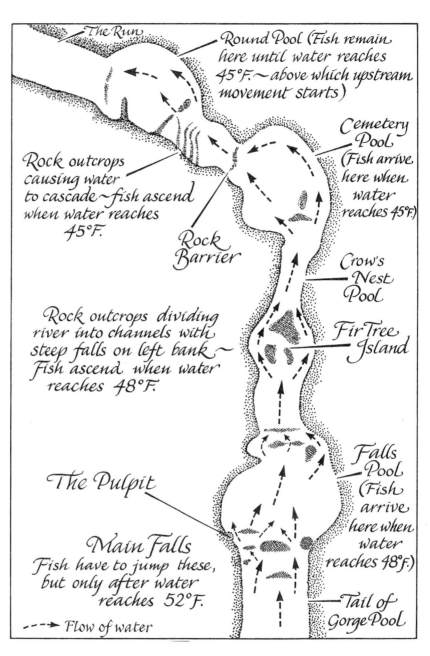

The Run

Round Pool (Fish remain here until water reaches 45°F. ~ above which upstream movement starts)

Rock outcrops causing water to cascade ~ fish ascend when water reaches 45°F.

Cemetery Pool (Fish arrive here when water reaches 45°F.)

Rock Barrier

Crow's Nest Pool

Rock outcrops dividing river into channels with steep falls on left bank ~ Fish ascend when water reaches 48°F.

Fir Tree Island

The Pulpit

Falls Pool (Fish arrive here when water reaches 48°F.)

Main Falls Fish have to jump these, but only after water reaches 52°F.

- - - → Flow of water

Tail of Gorge Pool

Salmon pools at the Cassley Falls showing water temperatures above which salmon will move upstream.

Shearer, using an electronic fish counter on the River North Esk (see next chapter) also recorded fish moving upstream after sunset. I, and many others, also recorded fish moving during the day both in clear and low water conditions. In Iceland it was found that salmon in the River Ellidaar migrated in dense runs during the night.

Menzies considered, as had Calderwood, the sea migrations of salmon and their possible feeding grounds in his Buckland Lectures for 1947 entitled *The Stock of Salmon: Its Migrations, Preservation and Improvement*. He drew attention to the fact that British and Norwegian records of recaptures of tagged salmon at sea indicated that many had travelled up to 1600 miles. Similarly, Canadian records revealed that salmon of the Gulf of St. Lawrence region also travelled considerable distances. It therefore seemed that salmon from rivers in countries on both sides of the Atlantic could possibly have a common sea feeding area. Menzies pointed out that salmon from both sides of the Atlantic live and feed under very similar conditions and, even if not on the same feeding ground, are subject to the same factors as is shown by the similarity in the variations in the catch. Menzies suggested that if salmon frequent feeding grounds up to 2,000 miles away from their native river, no physical difficulty would prevent all salmon frequenting the same feeding area. Menzies pointed out that much of the Atlantic Ocean between Iceland and Greenland is within the range of salmon from both North America and Europe. How right he was proved to be! Dr Huntsman in eastern Canada was asking the same question when he said "Where do salmon caught in Greenland go?" Although he was of the opinion that salmon remain within the vicinity of their parent river.

From the 1930's the interest in salmon in the universities increased and a significant number of contributions were made, particularly on the juvenile stages. Dr Bull of the University of Newcastle recorded a number of observations on the descent of smolts on the River Tyne. He suggested from his observations on the descent of smolts on the River Tyne that a small spate caused by a tenth of an inch of rain falling locally may be sufficiently effective to stimulate smolts to commence their downstream movement. Local conditions, however,

Parasitic maggots on the gills of a salmon

can vary and other stimuli may be more effective. Dr White in 1939, working in eastern Canada, found that the descent of smolts was determined by a rise in temperature and low light intensity, not by rainfall or rise in water level. However, a number of observations have been made of smolt migration on a number of rivers and the factors influencing migration vary. Dr Solomon recorded the smolt run to start in earnest once the water temperature remained above 10°C. However, the general conclusion is that smolts move downstream in the spring and a rise in water temperature is probably a stimulus and the onset of a flood will affect their ability to hold station and they will drop downstream. My own observations include watching smolts approaching and dropping over a waterfall, tail first, on a warm spring day. My later experiments record some of the conditions prevailing at the time of migration.

Mr Friend of Edinburgh University was, in 1941, unravelling the life-cycle of the salmon gill maggot, *Salmincola salmonea*. The adult salmon is infected by the parasite while in the river and it remains on the gills of the fish on its return to sea. Fish returning to the river to spawn again usually carry the parasite, although not always, and therefore it is possible, from the presence of these parasites to recognise a fish that had previously spawned.

In the early 1930's Berg in North America described the spawning habits of salmon, and Dr Jack Jones of Liverpool University also undertook interesting work on the spawning of salmon during the late 1940's and early 1950's. His observations of the spawning act were made in tanks constructed on the banks of the River Alwen, a tributary of the Welsh Dee. He describes some of his work in his excellent New Naturalist Monograph, *The Salmon,* published in 1959. One experiment of particular interest involved parr spawning with an adult female salmon and in the presence of a sterilized male adult salmon. The hen fish was prevented from covering her eggs with gravel. The eggs were transferred in separate batches to a hatchery where they were kept separate. By the following March 2,436 of the 2,504 eggs were eyed, giving a fertilization rate of 97.7%. Dr Jones had those spawnings, and others, filmed. The filming of spawning salmon, albeit in tanks, was a great advance and it was to be some years later before John Webb and Alan Youngson would describe the spawning acts of salmon in the wild in a tributary of the Aberdeenshire Dee.

In the early 1930's the fish disease furunculosis was prevalent in Scotland during the summer months in low water conditions. Government scientists investigated the disease and the Furunculosis Committee submitted two interim reports in 1930 and 1933 published by HMSO. Dr Isobel Smith working for the Department of Agriculture and Fisheries for Scotland in Aberdeen gave considerable attention to this disease some years later. She also recorded its presence in kelts.

Throughout the 1940's and 50's a number of studies were made of the growth and feeding habits of salmon parr. In 1940 K Carpenter recorded the food of parr in the Welsh Dee. She found that salmon parr were indiscriminately carnivorous and that their diet varied in close accord with the number and relative accessibility of the species of food present. A marked seasonal cycle in feeding was observed, which seemed to be directly dependent on the various life-cycles of the food organisms. Winifred Frost and Arthur Went investigated the growth and feeding habits of young salmon as part of the River Liffey investigations in Ireland and KR Allen studied the growth and feeding habits of the early stages of salmon in the River Eden in Westmorland and the Thurso River in Sutherland. Their findings were published in the scientific literature.

Further investigations were undertaken in Ireland and Arthur Went in his Buckland Lectures entitled *Irish Salmon and Salmon Fisheries* in 1955 gives an account of the natural history of Irish salmon and the movements of salmon around the Irish coast. There is evidence from these experiments that fish travelling to the same river shoal together in the sea, since fish tagged at the same time were recaptured in the same river, often within a short period of time of each other. He concluded that salmon do travel long distances at comparatively high speeds along the Irish coasts and even to parts of the coastline of Great Britain.

In eastern Canada and Newfoundland government scientists were involved in salmon investigations. AG Huntsman investigated the periodic scarcity of salmon and produced an interesting report on cyclical abundance and 'birds versus salmon' based on observations from salmon rivers in the maritime region of Canada. Over this period there was concern over the predation of young salmon by mergansers and belted kingfishers and HC White produced a number of interesting government publications on the subject.

With an expansion in industry after the Second World War there was an urgent need for power and this resulted in hydropower development in the Highlands of Scotland. This entailed the harnessing of many of Scotland's major rivers with a consequent construction of dams and pipelines and the formation of reservoirs. These were inevitably going to have an effect on salmon populations.

Water pollution had been affecting salmon populations throughout much of their geographic range. Salmon were no longer returning to the rivers Thames, Mersey, Clyde and Carron to name but a few and their numbers had diminished in the Tyne. Calderwood referred to river pollution in *Salmon and Sea Trout* in 1930. At that time it seems that the most important pollutants were sewage, lead from mines, bitumen from roads and sugar beet processing. Some years later other forms of pollution were also affecting salmon stocks. In Scotland pulp mill effluent had a marked effect on the water quality of the Aberdeenshire Don in particular. In Galloway increased afforestation by the Forestry Commission resulted in many waters becoming acidified and agricultural sprays and sheep dip had also become a problem. Salmon populations in other countries were also feeling the effects of various forms of pollution. In eastern Canada rivers such as the Miramichi were badly affected by DDT from the spraying of forests to eliminate spruce budworm. In Norway some rivers had become acidified from the effects of acid rain emanating from the acid-rich fumes arising from industrial areas considerable distances away.

The subject, as far as it concerned domestic and some forms of industrial pollution, had been addressed by a number of scientists and FTK Pentelow had raised the subject of river purification in his Buckland Lectures on this subject in 1952.

Government scientists were therefore going to be increasingly involved in salmon studies that would help alleviate some of these problems. In Scotland the Brown Trout Research Laboratory that was founded in the late 1940's was renamed in January 1957 the Freshwater Fisheries Laboratory with a remit that involved not only existing brown trout studies but also salmon investigations centred initially on the Aberdeenshire Dee.

In England there was only a small government staff responsible for salmon work but local fishery authorities were engaged in salmon research locally and their involvement was therefore going to be of increasing value.

A Salmon Research Group was set up at this time and consisted of scientists engaged in salmon research in the British Isles, including Ireland, with guest fishery biologists from Sweden, Norway and Iceland. An invaluable résumé of the literature on salmon studies was undertaken by KA Pyefinch of the Freshwater Fisheries Laboratory at Pitlochry and published by the Scottish Home Department in 1955. This reference work helped newly appointed fisheries staff focus on gaps in our knowledge of salmon.

As a result of the tagging of salmon that had been stripped of their eggs at Loch na Croic on the River Blackwater for incubation in the Contin Hatchery near Strathpeffer in Ross-shire future developments in salmon research were going to change. One of the fish that had been stripped and then tagged on release at this site in 1955 was recaptured off the West Coast of Greenland in 1956. Menzies' speculation was correct! In the following years salmon tagged in England, Wales, France, and Canada as well as Scotland were recovered in the burgeoning salmon fishery off West Greenland by fishing vessels not only from Greenland but also from Denmark, Germany and the Faroes. There was also a drift-net salmon fishery off the north Norwegian coast and a developing long-line salmon fishery off the Faroes. The pressure on salmon stocks returning to home waters therefore increased dramatically. Furthermore, in Scotland, they were also under pressure from the new hydro-electric schemes in the Scottish Highlands, poisoning of salmon in many rivers by gangs of poachers, and the imminent illegal drift-netting of salmon off the Scottish east coast. In addition there were drift-net salmon fisheries off the west coast of Ireland and the northeast coast of England. Eastern Canada, too, was having difficulties with its aboriginal fisheries. Partly as a consequence of these developments a number of salmon investigations were set up that involved more sophisticated equipment and teamwork. The next chapter describes the work involved and interesting developments.

CHAPTER THREE

Advances in Salmon Research

In order to learn more about the salmon life-cycle, an understanding of the underlying conditions influencing population fluctuations and factors affecting local survival monitoring both juvenile and adult salmon stocks was essential. Such a requirement entailed interrupting the migrations of both the juvenile and adult populations on their migrations and setting up a census of juveniles while resident in their nursery areas. A note of their abundance while in residence is undertaken by means of electro-fishing. The migration of the sea-going juveniles and returning adults can be recorded if it is possible to install a suitable trap.

One of the first traps used in Scotland was installed in the late 1950's on the Lui Burn, a small tributary stream of the Aberdeenshire Dee near Braemar. Its purpose was to enable a record of the survival of salmon fry that hatched from eyed eggs planted in the streams in slatted perspex boxes known as Vibert boxes (named after the well-known French fisheries biologist, Dr Richard Vibert). All migrating fry and parr were caught as they were swept over a horizontal wire mesh screen into a trough, fed with water at one end and led into a holding box. The stream was also electro-fished to determine the density of the resident fry and parr population. The experiment was part of the research programme of the Freshwater Fisheries Laboratory at Pitlochry.

A major salmon research scheme was established on the River

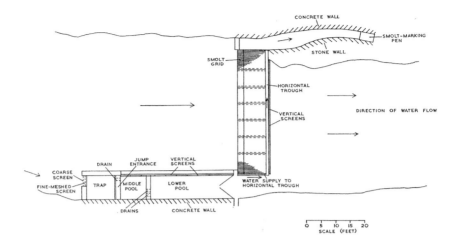

Diagram of the horizontal grid trap and pools for ascending and descending fish

Conon system in Ross-shire in 1956. Its programme and progress were the responsibility of a Salmon Research Committee consisting of members of the North of Scotland Hydro-electric Board, the Scottish Home Department and the Conon Salmon District Fishery Board. Its daily work was in the hands of a delegated staff member of the Pitlochry Freshwater Fisheries Laboratory who was in local residence near Strathpeffer and in charge of the new Salmon Research Laboratory in Contin. The responsibility for this was mine.

Two horizontal grid type traps were installed on the River Conon system, one on the Conon immediately below the Conon Falls and Luichart dam and reservoir, above which was the River Bran, and one on the River Meig. Both traps were sited a short distance below the hydro-electric dams and the impounded reservoirs. The purpose of this scheme was to compare the smolt production on the Meig, in which river the salmon spawned naturally, with the smolt production on the River Bran into which were released unfed salmon fry reared in the Contin Hatchery from eggs stripped from salmon trapped on the River Blackwater at Loch na Croic, another tributary of the Conon, that had had its upper reaches and spawning grounds diverted to another part of the river system. The traps were constructed to enable both the descending smolts and ascending adults to be trapped. HMSO published the early results of this scheme. To give some idea of the numbers of fish being handled, and recorded and, in the case of the smolts, tagged. The numbers of smolts recorded at the Meig trap in the first three years of operation (1957–59) were 13,943, 9,047 and 10,367. The numbers of ascending adults trapped over the same period on the Meig were 613, 254 and 246. The numbers of fish descending as kelts over these three years were 151, 28 and 25, which corresponds to 24.6, 10.9 and 10.2% of the upstream run. The upstream runs of adult fish in the three years 1965–67 were considerably higher at 829, 549 and 835 respectively. The main period of upstream migration was mid-July to mid-September. There can be changes in the pattern of run-timing though and Dr Summers showed that parallel long-term changes in run-timing were evident in the patterns of catches since the middle of the nineteenth century.

It was interesting to record, and confirm, the earlier observations of Calderwood and Menzies, of a significant increase in the downstream movement of parr in the autumn, most of which were ripe males. Alan Youngson and David Hay recorded an autumn downstream movement of parr at their trap on the Girnock Burn and they discuss this movement in *The Lives of Salmon*. Some of the parr were ripe males, others were not. They found from tagging studies that the immature males in the autumn were moving purposefully towards the sea, in the van of next year's smolt migration. The mature males reflected the movements these fish undertake in their attempts to reach and spawn with sexually mature adult females. Youngson and Hay showed that it had become possible to examine the role of the parr in spawning using new genetic techniques. As a group it was found that mature male parr are reasonably successful in siring progeny and they cover many of the females' eggs. This discovery had been made possible by the recent development of single-locus genetic probes. These probes were a development of the DNA 'fingerprinting' techniques.

A fry trap on one of the experimental streams.

To return to the results on the Conon, it was found that far fewer smolts and adults were recorded at the trap below the Conon Falls and the results suggested that there could be a number of environmental factors operating on the Bran that were affecting smolt production. This led to an independent investigation that I was delegated to conduct.

An assessment was made of the population density of young salmon in the Bran using electrical fishing methods and it was estimated that the average number of 1 and 2 year old smolts was about 7.3 per 100 square yards which was similar to that recorded for other tributaries of the Meig and Conon (7.6), and to the Pollett River in Canada. A value of 7.3 per 100 square yards indicated that the total parr population throughout the study area was 37,000. The average length of the fry at the end of their first year was 5.0cm, similar to those in the River Forss and Thurso in Caithness.

The food of the salmon fry was the nymphs of mayflies and stoneflies during the winter, water fleas (cladocera) during the late summer, caddis fly larvae during the autumn and midge larvae throughout the year. The food of the parr was similar to that of the fry though they also fed on salmon fry, particularly in the spring just after they had been released.

A detailed study was made of fry survival in two streams that had horizontal screen fry traps erected close to their confluence with the main river. It was found that there was a downstream movement of fry that took place within the first five weeks of planting and that the daily downstream movement of fry increased with a rise in water level and a consequent increase in flow. The mortality in the streams was high and the survival to the underyearling stage ranged from 0.2 to 2.6% of the unfed fry released. The heavy mortalities were probably due to the high rate of stocking by the staff of the district fishery board and to predation by small trout and parr.

The smolt migration from the Bran was monitored with box traps attached to a wooden bridge spanning the river close to the lochs on the lower reaches of the river. In the three years in which sampling took place migration was found to start after the water temperature was consistently above 10°C. Downstream movement took place at an average rate of approximately 0.5 miles (0.8km) to 0.7 miles (1.12km) per day. The age composition of the runs varied slightly each year. In one year (1960) about 64% of the migrants were two years old and 36% three years old; in the next two years (1961 and 1962) the corresponding proportions were 52% and 48%. Favourable weather conditions during the summer 1959 may have been the reason for the high proportion of two-year old smolts in 1960.

The estimated smolt production from the Bran was 18,600 in

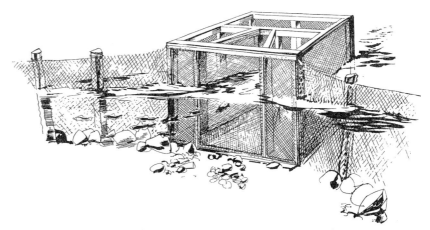

A box trap fixed in the river to intercept migrating smolts.

1961 and 17,500 in 1962. A comparison of these estimates with the numbers of unfed fry stocked in earlier years indicates that survival from the unfed fry stage to the smolt stage was 2.4% in 1961 and 3.1% in 1962. Smolt production therefore was very similar to that of the Pollett River in New Brunswick.

Predators of young salmon in the River Bran and associated lochs included pike, trout, goosanders, and black-headed and common gulls. Over 3,000 pike stomachs were examined and from the results it was estimated that on the two lochs into which the Bran flows the proportion of pike consuming smolts was between 16% and 37%. A mean estimate indicated that pike predation accounted for a tenth of the smolt run.

The investigation showed that a satisfactory number of smolts can be produced in a river such as the Bran from plantings of about 700,000 unfed fry. There was evidence that this planting was too high, e.g. 18,600 smolts were produced in 1961 from plantings of some 750,000 unfed fry but in the following year 550,000 unfed fry produced some 17,400 smolts.

Although the smolt production was satisfactory there would always be a problem of high mortality from predation, and delay at a barrage, two dams and two reservoirs if the smolts were left to

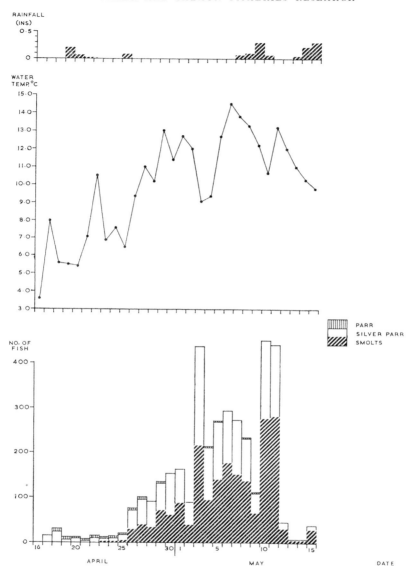

The smolt migration from the River Bran, 1962.
(The lower histograms depict the numbers of parr, silvering parr and smolts caught in the box traps each day; the graph records daily water temperature and the upper histograms rainfall)

move downstream on their own accord. It was therefore decided to transport them from the traps on the Bran after they had been tagged, and release them in the River Conon below the lowermost dam at Tor Achilty on the Conon. Over a period from 1963 to 1966 a total of 10,482 smolts was transported from the lower reaches of the River Bran and released in the lower reaches of the River Conon. Practically all, 99.8%, of the smolts survived. The percentage of smolts recaptured as adult fish from 1963 to 1966 experiments were 2.8, 2.2, 2.2 and 4.0% respectively. The recapture of tagged fish in other tributaries of the river system indicated that there was a certain amount of straying. The results from these initial experiments justified the transport of smolts from the River Bran becoming an annual management practice and since 1963 to this day smolts have been transported successfully from the Bran. In order to trap the majority of smolts under a range of water levels a permanent trap was installed. As a result of this management practice adult fish now spawn in the Bran which has now become a significant salmon river when, prior to the early 1960's, it was inaccessible to salmon. The first salmon to be caught by an angler on the Bran was in 1960.

Ascending salmon and returning kelts are counted at a number of the dams on the rivers harnessed by the North of Scotland Hydro-electric Board. They include the Tummel at Pitclochry, the Inverness-shire Garry at Invergarry, the Beauly at Kilmorack and Aigas, the Conon at Tor Achilty, the Meig at Loch Meig, and the Shin at Lairg

Calderwood had suggested that some salmon probably stray into other rivers on their return migration and Huntsman discussed wandering versus homing in a paper to the *Salmon and Trout Magazine* in 1952. From the results of the smolt transport experiments and from the tagging of smolts at the Meig and Conon Falls traps there was evidence of some straying. Ninety percent of the fish recaptured were within the Conon River system by anglers and at trapping sites or in neighbouring coastal nets, while the remaining 10% were taken in Greenland waters.

Between 1965 and 1971 similar surveys to that undertaken on the River Bran were made on the River Axe in Devon by the Devon

River Authority. Here the smolt migration was monitored at a trap similar in construction to those on the Meig and Conon.

The Pitlochry Freshwater Fisheries Laboratory in 1966 started a research scheme on the Girnock Burn, a tributary of the Aberdeenshire Dee. The trapping facilities were similar to those on the Rivers Meig and Conon and ascending adult fish and descending smolts and kelts were recorded. It was possible to keep a fairly close check on the adults when they were upstream of the trap and make careful observations of their spawning behaviour. These observations, entailing long hours by the waterside, were undertaken by John Webb, David Hay and Alan Youngson. Detailed accounts of spawning in the Girnock Burn are described in *The Lives of Salmon* by Youngson and Hay.

At about this time (i.e. the late 1960's and early 1970's) there was a serious outbreak of the salmon disease that had occurred in the late 1890's and early 1900's and been documented by Malloch at that time. The outbreak in the 1960's was more serious, but probably the recording of incidents was better recorded in the 1960's.

The disease this time was referred to as ulcerative dermal necrosis or UDN. The pattern of the spread of the disease was similar. The disease was first recorded in epidemic proportions in a number of rivers in southwest Ireland in 1964–65. During 1966 the disease spread to the Lancashire, Cumberland and Solway river systems and by the end of 1967 it had spread to all east coast Scottish rivers from the Tweed to the Nairn with the exception of the Forth and Tay and, on the west coast from the Solway Firth to the River Ayr. In 1968 cases appeared in the Forth, Tay, Ness and Conon river systems. The first signs of this disease are the appearance of small bleached areas of the skin on the head, back and near the dorsal fin and on the tail. As the disease progresses areas of bluish-grey, slimy growth develop on these bleached areas, making the fish very conspicuous in the water. As the disease spreads more patches appear and others spread so that considerable areas over the head and back are affected. Dr Elson, a specialist in fish disease at the Aberdeen Marine Laboratory, from his examination of fish from the tidal reaches of the River Tweed, suggested that some fish are infected with UDN before they reach fresh water.

A salmon heavily infested with UDN.

While the work to isolate the causative organism of UDN went on the numbers of infected salmon in Scottish rivers rose and from March 1967 to February 1968 a total of 41,234 infected salmon were removed from Scottish rivers. This total amounted to 12.6% of the provisional Scottish salmon catch for 1967 by all methods.

Dr Munro, a bacteriologist at the Aberdeen Marine Laboratory, pointed out that many high annual catches were made over the period of the outbreak in the nineteenth century, indicating that the species was never in danger of extinction; indeed the disease may have occurred as a result of an exceedingly large population. Munro considered that similar factors might have operated to start the present outbreak, though available information was too meagre to draw such a conclusion.

The disease also affected sea-trout and, to a much lesser extent, other freshwater fish.

Cases of UDN reported became less over the ensuing years and few fish are now reported with UDN.

A major salmon research scheme was set up in the late 1960's on the River North Esk run by staff of the Freshwater Fisheries Laboratory at Pitlochry based at its Montrose Field Station and supervised by Mr Willie Shearer. The North Esk is one of Scotland's major salmon rivers and the data collected from such a river was going to be invaluable, particularly as a commercial salmon netting company, Joseph Johnston's, based at Montrose with their salmon fixed engines sited in Montrose Bay and their sweep netting stations operating on the North Esk, was able to check the salmon they caught for fish marked at the Kinnaber research facility.

In *The Atlantic Salmon: Natural History, Exploitation and Future Management,* based on his Buckland Lectures for 1989, Shearer describes the trapping facilities on the North Esk. The smolt trap was initially installed at Kinnaber Waterworks and later a trap for both smolts and adults was constructed at the former Kinnaber Mill. An automatic fish counter to monitor migrating fish was erected at Logie, 6 km from the sea. It consisted of a three-channel, two stage, compound Crump weir. The weir comprised trench sheeting foundations embedded in the gravel substrate of the river and pre-formed glass-reinforced plastic (GRP) deck sections supported on triangular steel bearers. Initially (until 1986) three resistivity counters were used, one to each section of the three-channel weir. Since 1986 a Logie fish counter has been used. These facilities enabled all fish ascending the river to be counted. Tests using CCTV apparatus have shown that the reliability of the counter exceeds 95% for upstream and downstream migrants. Such sophisticated research facilities on a major salmon river, where practically the entire run of adult salmon could be monitored, resulted in excellent data that were transformed into important communications in the scientific literature written by Shearer, Dunkley and MacLean. In his book Shearer gives a useful table giving the estimated annual smolt production and numbers of salmon returning to home waters (the North Esk) from the smolt years 1964–68, 71–6, 80–2, and 84–5. Such data are most useful for fishery managers working on similar rivers and needing such information to help them estimate the size of their smolt and adult migrations.

One thinks back to the coastal tagging of adult salmon by Calderwood and Menzies when one looks at the figures in Shearer's book depicting the recapture sites of adult salmon tagged and released from coastal nets on the west coast, northwest coast, north coast, north-east coast and in the Moray Firth over the period of approximately 1952–88. Shearer has been able to go one step further with his results and has estimated the exploitation rates of the fixed engines (bag nets and stake nets), net and coble, and rod and line. Exploitation rates in the North Esk over the period 1976–88 were 35–62% for grilse and 30–63% for salmon. Dr Gersham Kennedy recorded much higher marine exploitation rates for the River Bush in Northern Ireland. His figures for wild microtagged grilse captured in the Irish drift-net fishery and Northern Ireland's drift and bag-net fishery ranged from 65.3–89.0%

Effort being put into salmon research projects throughout the geographic range of the salmon continued to increase and a number of trusts, societies and charities devoted to the welfare of this fish were established. In Canada and the USA there was the Atlantic Salmon Association that merged with the International Atlantic Salmon Foundation to become the Atlantic Salmon Federation. France established L'Association de Défense du Saumon Atlantique and in the United Kingdom the Salmon and Trout Association had been in existence for many years. However, in 1967 due to the escalating Greenland salmon fishery, the salmon mortalities from UDN and the increase in poaching, interested parties in the UK formed the Atlantic Salmon Research Trust that, after a short while, changed its title to the Atlantic Salmon Trust.

The first major assembly of Atlantic salmon biologists, administrators, conservationists and politicians was convened at a symposium in St. Andrews, New Brunswick, Canada in 1972. This was a significant gathering of like-minded individuals. As Wilfred Carter, chairman of the International Atlantic Salmon Foundation says in his introduction to the Symposium proceedings:

> More than 400 students, scientists, conservationists and fishermen from 12 different countries attended the three-day conference, contributing to the articulate dialogue evoked by many of the stimulating papers presented.

A miscellany of papers delivered at this symposium demonstrated the direction in which salmon research was moving. There were sessions on politics, physiology, ecology and conservation. The effects man was having on the salmon's freshwater environment were demonstrated loud and clear and it was an indication in which direction future work should concentrate. Drs Carter and Smith edited the proceedings under the title *Proceedings of the International Symposium on the Atlantic Salmon: Management, Biology and Survival of the Species,* published by the International Atlantic Salmon Foundation and the Atlantic Salmon Research Trust.

A number of investigations along these lines had already been started particularly with regard to hydroelectric power development, water resources, afforestation, acid rain and pollution from pulp mills. I had already drawn attention to these matters in my recently published book *Salmon and Trout: A Resource, its Ecology, Conservation and Management* (1971). The book was partly designed to help students attending my honours degree course in fisheries management in the Department of Forestry & Natural Resources in the University of Edinburgh.

Salmon research projects were now very much part of the management programmes of the government laboratories and English river authorities and there was growing concern over the West Greenland salmon fishery.

It was therefore not a surprise when a second salmon symposium was organised by the Atlantic Salmon Trust and International Atlantic Salmon Foundation and held in Edinburgh in 1976. Although the present status, health, ecological constraints and future management of salmon stocks in the Atlantic salmon producing countries was the major subject of this symposium, the present situation with regard to the salmon's future and related political issues were also of prime importance and were to become significant. The subject of salmon farming also reared its head as, although of little significance at that time, the alarm bell was close to sounding. No-one at that time, I'm sure, realised how controversial the whole subject of salmon farming would become.

The most important result arising from the symposium was the proposal for the setting up of a North Atlantic Salmon Convention. This took the form of a resolution. The main part of the resolution resolved that for effective protection of North Atlantic salmon and in order to encourage the rehabilitation and enhancement of Atlantic salmon wherever they are found or once occurred, and for the national management of salmon fisheries, an International Convention for Atlantic Salmon be established by those countries bordering the North Atlantic and its connected seas that produce and/or fish for Atlantic salmon. The Symposium further resolved that such convention should include, *inter alia,* provisions to:

1. Ban fishing for Atlantic salmon beyond 12 miles;
2. Provide for co-operation among all countries in conservation, regulation and enforcement measures and
3. Provide a forum for international co-operation in research and the exchange of data on Atlantic salmon.

The resolutions were put to the Symposium and passed unanimously.

These resolutions bore fruit and a few years later became the North Atlantic Conservation Organisation (NASCO).

The proceedings of the symposium, entitled *Atlantic salmon: its future*, were edited by Dr Went and published by Fishing News Books in 1980.

More attention was now being paid to the Greenland drift-net fishery. Canada found that this fishery was taking very many of its fish. For example, in one Quebec experiment it was found that 42% of tagged smolts were taken in Greenland, 42% in Newfoundland and only 16% in home waters. A detailed statistical study of returning tagged fish from New Brunswick and Nova Scotia indicated that the Greenland fishery may have taken as much as 27–38% of large salmon and 32–68% of Nova Scotia large salmon. The same concern was shown by countries bordering the north-eastern Atlantic and fish tagged in the home waters of the United Kingdom, the Republic of Ireland, France, Norway and Spain were also being caught in this fishery. Furthermore, a small team of scientists from the UK and Canada visited Greenland to inspect the fishery and tag and

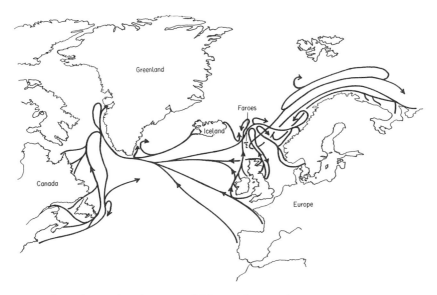

Approximate migration routes of Atlantic salmon in the north Atlantic area

release salmon taken by commercial vessels. Some of these tagged fish were subsequently caught in home waters. In 1971 the landings from this fishery soared to 2,689 tonnes. Following several years of persistent state and private effort, the International Commission for the Northwest Atlantic Fisheries (ICNAF) established in 1972 a quota for this fishery of 1,191 metric tons per annum, simultaneously phasing out the high seas foreign drift-net fishery by Faroese, Swedish and German vessels. In future the fishery was to be operated only by Greenland boats and within the 12-mile fishery limits.

Although there had been a very small floating long-line fishery for salmon close to the Faroe Islands the total annual landings from this fishery up until 1971 were no more than 40 tonnes. However, following the introduction of economic zones (i.e. within the new 200 mile zone) the salmon fishery increased rapidly and the major portion of the catch was made some distance to the north of the islands. Salmon tagged as smolts in Norway, Sweden, Scotland, England and Ireland were caught as adult salmon in this fishery. A number of salmon caught commercially were also tagged and released

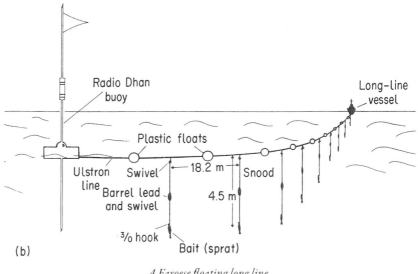

A Faroese floating long line.

by fishery scientists accompanying the boats and a number of these tagged fish were later recaptured in home water fisheries.

In 1980 it was arranged that a small team of scientists representing the Atlantic Salmon Trust and International Atlantic Salmon Foundation visit Greenland to inspect the arrangements for observing the quota imposed and to discuss general matters with the Greenland fishermen, government officials and to inspect the fishery. The results of the visit were published by the Atlantic Salmon Trust as a *Report of the Joint Greenland Expedition (1980)* (compiled by Henrik Kreiberg). This resulted in a friendly understanding of the management of the Greenland fishery with an imposed quota. However, as we shall see later, arrangements over quotas would change dramatically.

A similar visit was made in 1982 to the Faroes with the consent of the Faroese government that was continuing to operate a floating long-line fishery for salmon. This fishery had been escalating from a catch of 718 tonnes in 1980 to 970 tonnes in 1981 with the threat of a further increase in 1982. The visit included discussions with the Prime Minister, the Minister of Fisheries, the Attorney-at-Law,

Line-caught salmon at Torshavn fish market.

and the chairman of the Fishermen's Association. As in Greenland, the visit was most amicable and the delegation was entertained to a banquet given in its honour at which the Prime Minister paid tribute to our associations, and to which I replied. A report on this visit was published in 1982 by the Atlantic Salmon Trust entitled *Report on a Visit to the Faroes* by Derek Mills and Noel Smart. It was agreed by our committees that both visits (to Greenland and the Faroes) had been a great success in paving the way for more official discussions.

As with the situation in Greenland, things were to change with the advent of the North Atlantic Conservation Organisation (NASCO). In 1982 NASCO was established in Reykjavik under the Convention for the Conservation of Salmon in the North Atlantic Ocean. Two years later, in January 1984, the organisation held its inaugural meeting in Edinburgh. The parties to the convention were: Canada; Denmark in respect of Greenland and the Faroe Islands; European Union; Iceland; Norway; Russia and the United States of America. Iceland has since left the organisation for reasons of economy. The organisation consists of a council, three regional commissions and a secretary. The commissions are the North American Commission, the North-east Atlantic Commission and the West Greenland Commission. NASCO's objective is to contribute through consultation and co-operation to the conservation, restoration, enhancement and rational management of salmon stocks, taking into account the best scientific evidence available to it. At the Annual Meetings of NASCO in its early years the size of quotas for both the Greenland and Faroese salmon fisheries were of most importance and frequently lengthy debates were held on these contentious issues.

It will be remembered from earlier in the text that Menzies hypothesised that salmon migrate long distances from the coast out into the north-eastern Atlantic or further, while Huntsman was of the reverse opinion and considered that they remained within the influence of the mouth of the river from which they originated. Since that time scientists, through their investigations on the high seas, have demonstrated that salmon are distributed seasonally over much of the northwest Atlantic and so make lengthy migrations far from their river of origin. A number of theories were suggested as to where in this region salmon occur. One thought was that it was in relatively cool water of 3° to 8° C. A little later other scientists demonstrated direct relationships between ocean climate, principally sea surface-temperature, and the abundance and distribution of salmon. Furthermore, Reddin and Shearer showed that salmon could modify their migratory path depending on the temperature of the water that they must swim through. In summary, they stated that salmon of all sea ages occurred seasonally over most of the northwest Atlantic and could be found concentrated in the Labrador Sea gyre throughout the year, at West Greenland in summer and autumn, and in the spring along the eastern slope of the Grand Bank.

Faroese scientists tracked both the horizontal and vertical movements of salmon. The vertical movements were tracked using depth-sensitive tags. It was found that, after release, all salmon dived very rapidly to a depth of more than 100 metres, most probably due to stress from handling and tagging. From later results of tagging,

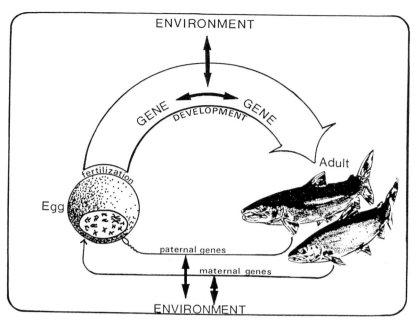

Schematic representation of the interaction of the genetic material of the egg with the environment to produce a salmon. Arrows indicate points of interaction.

salmon ascended slowly after the initial deep dive and reached the top 10 m surface layer 4 hours after release. One salmon tagged with an acoustic tag was tracked for 5.5 days. After the initial deep dive the fish ascended to a depth of approximately 40 m where it remained for the next 50 hours, interrupted by only irregular visits to the surface. Another salmon tracked had a tag that did not discriminate between depths of less than 12 m. This salmon after an initial dive remained above 12 m for most of the tracking period with irregular dives of short duration mostly down to 40 m but also one to 80 m and one to 120 m.

Swimming activity was also measured during the same experiments and the figures indicated periods of high activity followed by periods of low activity. The periods of low swimming activity were mostly recorded during the evening and the periods of high swimming activity mostly during the daytime.

Further results of these experiments were presented by Hjalti

Jákupsstovu at the Third International Atlantic Salmon Symposium held in Biarritz in 1986.

Two more presentations on the life of salmon at sea delivered at this symposium highlighted the need for more data on the sea-life of salmon if we were to understand and take precautions to conserve salmon stocks during the period in which they spent the greater part of their lives.

The proceedings of this symposium, entitled *Atlantic Salmon: Planning for the Future* and edited by David Piggins and Derek Mills, were published by Croom Helm in 1988.

Some attention has been paid in recent years to the genetics of salmon. In the early 1980's some geneticists had concluded that the Atlantic salmon could be divided genetically into a North American race and a European race. In Europe there exist at least two races, the 'celtic' and the 'boreal.' The Baltic salmon constitute a third distinct European race.

The geneticist Dr Eric Verspoor, in a talk at the *Tweed Towards 2000* conference, remarked that the genetic constitution of a salmon is determined by in the order if 10,000 to 100,000 functional sequences of DNA. These are the units of hereditary information commonly known as genes or genetic loci. Each genetic locus has a specific role in a complex interplay of genes. Each gene consists of two parts, known as alleles, that function separately and equally as components of the gene unit. This interplay dictates the development of the egg into a salmon, the salmon's physical character and behaviour, and its survival and reproductive success. From genetic studies it would be possible to trace the origin of fish that may have 'strayed' into another river tributary or river system. Salmon genetic studies were to become of importance when considering the effects of the breeding of escaped farm salmon with wild fish.

CHAPTER FOUR

Conservation And Management

The Atlantic salmon originally occurred in every country whose rivers flowed into the North Atlantic Ocean and Baltic Sea. In some instances the country had no coastline bordering either of these waters, for example Czechoslovakia, Luxembourg and Switzerland, and the salmon had to undergo long upstream migrations on such rivers as the Vltava (Czechoslovakia) and the Rhine (Luxembourg and Switzerland). Salmon have now disappeared from the rivers of these countries due to the erection of navigation locks, the construction of dams, and pollution.

Although these countries were the first to lose their salmon, other countries through which these and other large rivers, such as the Seine, Douro, Meuse and Thames, ran were soon to experience a similar loss as a result of water abstraction, impoundment and pollution. The same situation was experienced in North America for similar reasons, and salmon in the rivers of New York, New England and Maine such as the Housatonic, Connecticut, Merrimack and Penobscot, quickly dwindled as these waterways were harnessed for power and factory production of numerous commodities. There are copious records of rivers "teeming" with Atlantic salmon right up until the middle of the nineteenth century, with some of the more fortunate rivers holding an abundance of salmon up until more recent times.

Whichever country one cares to choose, with the possible exception of Iceland, the same story of dwindling stocks unfolds.

In the United Kingdom, the late nineteenth century brought with it increased river pollution, particularly of the lower reaches, and the Clyde, Tyne, Tees, Taff, Trent, Ribble and Ouse, to name but a few, fell victim to the thoughtless actions of polluters. Spain saw the demise of salmon in many of its rivers like the Mino and Naton through dam construction and excessive water abstraction for irrigation, while stocks dwindled almost to the point of extinction on the Dordogne, Garonne, Bresle, Gironde, and Loire from pollution and the construction of dams for mills and hydroelectric power. The salmon streams of Canada's provinces of Nova Scotia experienced the destruction of salmon stocks from logging activities, resulting in rapid run-off and excessively high water temperatures, while most of the north shore rivers of Quebec from the Sanguenay west to Lake Ontario, including the Jacques Cartier, became polluted and lost their salmon runs. Even Norway, a country renowned for the number and size of its salmon, did not escape the effects of industrialisation and pollution resulted in the loss of salmon from rivers such as the Akerselv and Drammenselv, while hydroelectric power has been a cause for concern for salmon stocks on rivers like the Laerdal. However, worse was to come.

In the early 1900s acidification as a result of sulphur dioxide emissions was starting to affect southern Norwegian rivers like the Tovdal and was responsible for the total loss of salmon from many of the rivers in southern Norway and the west coast of Sweden. It was also affecting rivers in southwest Scotland, mid-Wales and parts of eastern Canada. Since the Second World War major power developments in Norway, Scotland, Sweden and eastern Canada have resulted in further reductions in both salmon numbers and the salmon's environment. In Sweden, as a result of whole river systems being harnessed, the stocks of salmon previously supported by the rivers Indal, Angerman, Umeå and Luleå, and others have had to be maintained artificially by smolts reared in local hatcheries and released into the lower reaches of these rivers below the lowermost dam. In Scotland and Canada, too, some salmon spawning areas have been lost due to flooding by reservoirs and stocks have had to be maintained by hatchery production. Although the threat from river pollution is starting to abate as a result of better pollution legislation, acid rain, water abstraction, afforestation, land and arterial drainage schemes continue to be a threat to the survival of the salmon. In recent years salmon farming has had an impact on salmon populations through infestations of sea lice.

Anthony Netboy has written a detailed chronicle of these past disasters in the history of the salmon's distribution and welfare with some feeling in his books *The Atlantic Salmon: A Vanishing Species?* and *Salmon: The World's Most Harassed Fish.* A more recent book by Michael Wigan – *The Salmon. The Extraordinary Story of the King of Fish,* published by William Collins in 2013, has brought these matters up to date.

However, the story has not all been one of 'doom and gloom.' Stock enhancement of course has been practised as long as one cares to remember, and with varying success, but probably not as much as one might imagine from the millions of eggs, fry, parr and smolts planted out in rivers of many countries where salmon stocks have shown signs of dwindling. Poor survival of introduced stock was due in the past to lack of knowledge of the implications, some genetic, of such practices. Now the story is changing. We have more knowledge of fish genetics. There is also a greater environmental awareness generally and, as water quality improves, there is increasing pressure to protect the aquatic environment from various forms of land and water use, and to reinstate degraded rivers. Such actions were to be welcomed, and would be noted by Greenland and Faroese salmon fishermen who had been quick to point out to salmon-producing nations the polluted state of some of their rivers when the delegations from the Atlantic Salmon Trust and International Atlantic Salmon Foundation visited their countries.

In the United States, salmon rehabilitation was under way in the early 1960's on the Dennys, Aroostook, Sheepscot and Narraguagus in Maine, and by the mid-1960's plans to restore the Penobscot in Maine had been completed. In the early 1970's arrangements were well advanced for the restoration of the Connecticut and Merrimack in New England. Elsewhere at this time similar work had started. In France, the Bresle was the first stream to have salmon restored to its waters, although it would not be long before many more French rivers were successfully rehabilitated. At this time, also, restoration and improvement work was under way on a number of Newfoundland rivers including the Upper Terra Nova, Great Rattling Brook and Noel Paul's Brook. The late 1970's saw restoration work start on the Dordogne in France, the Drammenselv in Norway and the Morell, Nepisiguit, Jacques Cartier and Exploits River in Canada. By the following decade salmon rehabilitation was snowballing. Projects were starting in the early 1980's on the Tyne and Thames in England, on the Akerselv flowing through Norway's capital city, Oslo, and on the Point Wolfe River in Newfoundland. By the mid to late 80's the Taff, Torridge, Loire-Allier, Boyne and Meuse had joined the list and salmon were recorded straying into the Clyde and Trent whose water quality was beginning to improve.

A conference on the Restoration of Salmon Rivers (*La Restauration des Rivières a Saumons,* edited by M Thibault and R Billard) held in France in 1987 and entirely devoted to this subject indicated the need for those involved in rehabilitation work to get together to discuss mutual problems. However, it attracted little attention from those concerned with salmon rehabilitation in the United Kingdom and the Republic of Ireland. So, in discussions with the Atlantic Salmon Trust and the Institute of Fisheries Management, it was decided that strategies for the rehabilitation of salmon rivers would be an appropriate and timely subject for a joint conference. This was held in late November 1990 at the Linnean Society in London.

The conference was a great success and speakers covered the restoration of the rivers Tyne and Yorkshire Ouse in England, Dordogne in France, Jacques Cartier in Quebec, Taff in Wales, Morell River in Prince Edward Island, Nepisiguit in New Brunswick, the Drammenselv in Norway, and the rivers Clyde, Forth and Carron in Scotland. The talks were published as *Strategies for the Rehabilitation of Salmon Rivers* by the Linnean Society in 1991. A summary of the proceedings was also published in German by the

Lachs-und Meerfollen Sozietät e.V. to assist the organisations helping to restore salmon to the Rhine and its tributaries.

Interest in salmon research at this time tended to be centred on river rehabilitation and the marine life of the salmon. It was therefore not surprising that the theme for the Fourth International Atlantic Salmon Symposium held in 1992, this time back in St. Andrews, Canada, was *Salmon in the Sea and New Enhancement Strategies*.

While there was information on the marine distribution of adult salmon from the investigations of Drs Reddin and Friedland, mentioned elsewhere in the text, little was known of the movements of smolts once they left coastal waters. This gap in our knowledge was noted by the delegates and was something to be rectified.

Dr Dunbar of the Department of Meteorology at McGill University, Montreal, made an interesting approach to the varying abundance and distribution of salmon in his presentation, *Salmon at Sea: Oceanographic Oscillations*. For example, he attributed the change in the migration route of the sockeye salmon due to the El Niňo Southern Oscillation and referred to similar changes in the Atlantic Ocean caused by the Great Salinity Anomaly first recorded in 1968, so called due to changes in salinity. This had a major impact on a number of fisheries. Examples of these changes are well described by David Cushing in his book *Climate and Fisheries*.

Drs Dunbar and Thomson, in a historical literature study, concluded that salmon had been present and absent in west Greenland waters in the following sequence:

1576–86	Salmon probably present
1605–25	Salmon probably abundant
18th century	Salmon scarce
1806–12	Salmon present, perhaps abundant
1820–50	Salmon scarce
1890–1928	Salmon scarce
1928–31	Salmon observed in increasing numbers
1935–58	Salmon becoming more common
1958–present	Salmon very abundant

Dunbar went on to cite cyclical abundance in commercial landings of salmon on the east coast of Canada since 1910, There was a peak in 1930, a decline to 1955, followed by an increase in 1965. The low points on the curve are some 50 years apart, the high points about 35 years apart. Dr Huntsman published a record of the fluctuations in the Miramichi fishery that showed peaks for 1874 and 1952 a 50-year period. At the mouths of three rivers in Co. Kerry there was an increase in the average weight of salmon between 1900 and 1925, followed by a decline to 1960. During the same period the annual catch in numbers of fish showed the reverse pattern, indicating a change in the proportion of grilse in the catch, a phenomenon recorded in Scotland with grilse numbers reaching peaks in the 1960's.

Fluctuations in the abundance of animals in the arctic are well documented and many species such as the rock ptarmigan, arctic fox, snowshoe hare and polar bear are all subject to periodic fluctuations in numbers that are influenced by climate change.

Whether or not salmon numbers off west Greenland have been affected by continuing climate warming is difficult to know owing to the restriction on salmon fishing controlled by a strict quota system imposed by NASCO.

Dr Ken Whelan gave a timely presentation at this symposium. It concerned the decline of sea-trout in the west of Ireland: an indication of forthcoming marine problems for salmon? It referred to the problem of the premature return of smolts, severe infestation of smolts and kelts by juvenile sea lice, the presence of badly emaciated fish and a significant reduction in spawning stock. The cause of these problems was laid at the feet of the burgeoning salmon farms on Ireland's west coast. There was little evidence at the time that this was going to be a major problem in all those countries where salmon farming was developing. We were going to hear more about it at later symposia, at NASCO and in the general press.

Mr Orri Vigfusson from Iceland gave the final presentation in the section on *Salmon in the Sea*. He explained the workings of the Committee for the Purchase of Open Sea Salmon Quotas and described the setting up of the North Atlantic Salmon Fund (NASF).

The workings of NASF are now well-known, and to which many salmon anglers contribute to it either as individuals or through their clubs and associations.

The reconditioning of kelts was a subject in the section on *New Enhancement Strategies*. An attempt to recondition kelts in a swimming pool in Morecambe had been attempted many years ago by Dr Leslie Stewart of the Lancashire River Board with a modicum of success. Methods had now improved when undertaken by the Department of Fisheries and Oceans in Canada. The conclusion reached from the experiments undertaken had two potential end uses:

Enhancement
    (i) A proven technique as a source of hatchery broodstock
    (ii) A promising technique as a source of natural spawners.
Commercial
    (i) Large operations with sale of kelts as food, either fresh, frozen or smoked.
    (ii) small one-tank operations, with kelts consumed by owners.
    (iii) kelts supported artificial fisheries, either in private ponds or public rivers.

The Conon District Salmon Fishery Board in Ross-shire, Scotland undertook kelt reconditioning with success. In this experiment the kelts were reconditioned, fed and held in tanks until ready for stripping of their eggs in the autumn. Some kelts were held for more than two years with their eggs being taken two years in succession.

To go back in time a few years, although the impact was not felt immediately, there was a serious outbreak of a skin parasitic fluke, *Gyrodactylus salaris*, on salmon in Norwegian rivers. It was originally introduced to Norwegian salmon farms from resistant farm stock in Sweden. It subsequently spread to wild populations in many Norwegian rivers with devastating effect. Infestations were characterised by violent outbreaks often with thousands of parasites on a single fish which, combined with fungus attacks, resulted in the mass deaths of salmon parr. As a result the parasite reduced considerably the stocks of juvenile salmon in many Norwegian rivers.

Strict rules regarding the disinfecting of the fishing gear of anglers visiting the British Isles and the importation of live fish has so far prevented the introduction of the parasite to this country.

The proceedings of the Fifth International Atlantic Salmon Symposium held in Galway in 1997 (edited by Whoriskey and Whelan) contained the Norwegian and Scottish investigations into the distribution of smolts after leaving their rivers, when they are referred to as post-smolts. They were undertaken by Norwegian and Scottish scientists (Drs Shelton, Turrell and Holst) in the Norwegian Sea, the North Sea and in the north-east Atlantic to the west of Shetland and the Outer Hebrides in 1991 and 1996. They established that post-smolt salmon were consistently present near the surface in the north-east-running shelf edge current to the west of the Outer Hebrides. By July-August, post-smolts were found in the Norwegian Sea with the largest concentrations observed from 68°-72°N. Scale examination revealed that growth in the early weeks at sea is rapid and many of the stomachs contained herring, sand eels and blue whiting. These were the first open sea investigations to trace the movements of post-smolts and were most encouraging. There would be further investigations to follow on from these preliminary studies.

There are a number of salmon predators, some of more importance than others. Freshwater predators include the pike, trout, goosander, red-breasted merganser and cormorant. Dr Elson, in a study of the American merganser (our goosander), on a Canadian river estimated that the population density of this bird was about 1 bird per 6 acres but until the population density had been reduced to 1 bird per 18 acres control had little effect. Reduction of bird control below this level had an increasingly advantageous effect on smolt production down to a population density of 1 bird per 24 acres. In my study of the distribution of the goosander and red-breasted merganser in Scotland I found the population density of the goosander on the Rivers Bran and Meig to be 1 bird per 24 acres. This suggested that the goosander population on these Scottish rivers was at a level where, according to Elson, bird control should have an effect on smolt production.

In my study of the distribution and food of the cormorant in

Scotland I found that cormorants fishing on lochs fed chiefly on brown trout, perch and young salmon, in that order. Cormorants fishing on rivers fed on brown trout, young salmon and eels. They also fed on three-spined sticklebacks, flounders, pike and sea-trout. One cormorant was found with a kelt of some three pounds in its gullet. However, it was concluded that the bird was not a serious predator of salmon except under circumstances where smolts are present in large numbers on their downstream migration, as was recorded from an examination of cormorants shot at the mouth of the River Tweed.

Dr Vaughan Anthony, in reviewing the literature on salmon predators, counted over 50 predators on both sides of the Atlantic that fed on Atlantic salmon during at least one of the five stages of the salmon's life-cycle. At the egg stage he records goldeneye duck, brook trout, and salmon parr, to which I can add brown trout and grayling. The fry and young parr are susceptible to predation from large parr, brown trout, brook trout, eels, burbot, belted kingfisher and goosander, otter and mink, to name but a few; large parr and smolts are the prey of pike, trout, goosanders, red-breasted mergansers, otters, hooded crows, herring gulls, common gulls and black-headed gulls. On entering estuarine waters smolts are susceptible to predation from cod, saithe or coalfish, pollack, striped bass, garfish, cormorants, shags, gannets and puffins. Once in the open ocean a further group of predators are added to the growing list. They include cod, Greenland shark and ling. On returning to the firths, sea lochs and estuaries the salmon are the prey of bottle-nosed dolphin, and predation on returning salmon by these dolphins is a spectacular sight in the Moray Firth and has become a tourist attraction.

The practice of catch and release was just coming into vogue in an attempt to regulate the numbers of salmon being retained by anglers. There were many who were a little doubtful of its benefit, believing that fish released after being handled would die. On the River Tweed anglers were supplied with tags and an applicator so that they could tag their fish before its release and on subsequent capture a second time the number on the tag could be noted and sent to the Tweed Foundation so that a record could be made of the numbers of fish

The Future Is in Your Hands.

A catch and release badge issued by the Atlantic Salmon Federation to anglers who record the salmon they have released.

being caught a second time or more. The practice did not last long as little useful information was forthcoming. However, John Webb of the Atlantic Salmon Trust was able to provide evidence of a good survival of released fin-clipped fish on the Aberdeenshire Dee where the fin clips were still discernible on later recapture.

Three Canadian scientists examined the biological effects of catch and release in Atlantic salmon under a wide range of conditions, both in the field and the laboratory. Taken together, their results showed that the vast majority of salmon do survive to spawn following catch and release. The results also indicated that certain conditions such as extremely soft water, water temperatures above 22°C, or a recent transition from seawater to freshwater might increase the magnitude of the physiological disturbance and the probability of mortality following catch and release.

The gentle handling of the fish on capture and holding it in water until it has been examined and/or photographed probably is the safest practice to ensure the fish's subsequent survival.

CHAPTER FIVE

The 21ˢᵗ Century

Drs Holst, Turrell, Shelton and Julian MacLean had pointed out at a symposium in Galway in 1995 that over the last two decades salmon catches in the north-east Atlantic had fallen to a greater extent than could readily be accounted for by the levels and distribution of fishing effort. The results of studies in monitored rivers provided further evidence that there had been real reductions in the abundance of some salmon populations and further that these reductions appeared to result, not from lower smolt production but from poorer sea survival. This perception increased demands for more research on the marine phase of the salmon's life-cycle. It was considered that tracing the movements and survival of the young salmon in the critical weeks after leaving their rivers was of paramount importance. This subject, and that of the effects of marine salmon farms on wild Atlantic salmon, were the two major topics at the Sixth International Atlantic Salmon Symposium entitled *Salmon at the Edge* and held in Edinburgh in 2002.

However, before this gathering, and partly as a result of the Salmon Symposium, *Salmon in the Sea and New Enhancement Strategies,* held in St. Andrews, Canada, in 1992, it was agreed that a multinational workshop, to be organised jointly by the Atlantic Salmon Trust and the Atlantic Salmon Federation, should be held to increase further our knowledge of salmon in the sea in greater detail. At this workshop, held in December 1992, a number of studies were recommended including the development of survey and tracking methods and environmental studies including the extraction and collation of various satellite data and their relationship to salmon abundance. To this end a three-year project, funded by the Ministry of Agriculture, Fisheries and Food and the Molson Family Foundation was started in 1995 involving the Atlantic Salmon Trust, the Atlantic Salmon Federation, the European Space Agency and the Atlantic Centre for Remote Sensing of the Oceans in Nova Scotia to improve our knowledge of the effects of ocean conditions on Atlantic salmon using information from the European ERS-2 earth observation satellite.

Some of the results of this project were presented later at a two-day workshop held at the Freshwater Fisheries Laboratory, Pitlochry, in November 1998. Of particular concern, and central to discussions at this meeting, was the fact that the total nominal catch of Atlantic salmon had declined from a peak in excess of approximately 12,700 tonnes in 1973 to approximately 2,300 tonnes in 1997.

A simplified flow diagram (opposite) was presented at the commencement of this workshop to help focus on some of the issues that required consideration.

It has already been seen that temperature governs the sea distribution of salmon. It also affects the distribution of the salmon's food organisms, as does the nutrient status. It has been suggested that recent warming of the northeast Atlantic Ocean has affected the abundance of food organisms. It is thought that this has been due to the timing of their appearance that has changed by 4–5 weeks. The microscopic plants known as diatoms or phytoplankton are blooming earlier but the organisms or zooplankton that feed on them appear later after the diatom blooms have ended. This is probably due to the fact that the cold water forms of zooplankton that have moved further north with the changes in water temperature are being replaced by warm water species that don't appear until after the diatom blooms are over and not in the same abundance as the cold water forms that are most preferable as food items for the post-smolts.

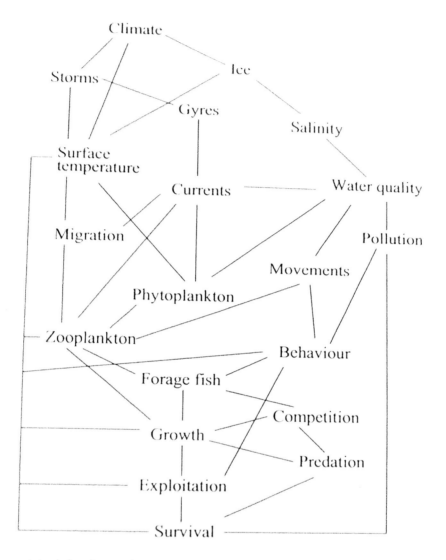

A simple flow diagram depicting marine environmental and biological factors influencing salmon survival.

A study of the food of post-smolts taken in coastal waters of Trondheim fjord revealed that insects appeared in about 60% of the fish stomachs and crustaceans in 93%. Fish remains were only present in 4%.

The food of salmon taken in oceanic waters consisted chiefly of fish and large planktonic organisms such as krill and amphipods (related to the sand-slaters found under dry seaweed on the beach). The fish species composition varied according to locality. For example, the chief fish species found in the stomachs of salmon caught on the Canadian Shelf were capelin, sand eels and herring, in that order; off West Greenland it was chiefly sand eels and capelin, while off the British Isles it was sand eels, herring and sprats.

Johannes Sturlaugsson, an Icelandic scientist, had this to say in his concluding remarks in his presentation on the food and feeding of salmon during feeding and spawning migrations in Icelandic coastal waters:

> The marine feeding migration of salmon is a survival combat in which the feeding conditions experienced are known to play a significant role, and the opportunistic feeding of salmon makes the best out of these circumstances. During the feeding migration, especially in the beginning, the feeding success of salmon is directly linked to their body growth. Therefore the successful feeders grow more rapidly 'out of trouble' than their counterparts, because at a critical period their larger body size will enhance their chance to survive e.g. to cope with diseases, predators and parasites and enable them to feed in colder water. The salmon that have for genetic or circumstantial reasons more successful feeding strategies and tactics have a head start in the race for survival. Here it must be remembered that post-smolts with diseases or parasitic infection above a certain level will, despite perfect feeding conditions, not survive.

It was shown that it was possible to track smolts once they had entered the sea and become post-smolts using a number of tracking methods involving tags such as archival or data storage tags and automated listening stations or acoustic tags and active tracking. On the evidence available from tagging and tracking experiments it appears that post-smolts from Ireland and possibly the west coast of Scotland enter the Slope Current, running north-east in the areas west of Scotland, and are transported first north and later north-eastwards past the Wyville-Thomson Ridge, through the Faroe-Shetland Channel into the Norwegian Sea. Post-smolts from the east coast of Scotland possibly follow the Dooley Current, which runs across the North Sea approximately from Aberdeen in a north-easterly direction heading towards the Norwegian coast after which they can enter the coastal current that runs northwards along the Norwegian coast. Alternative routes could take them through the Fair Isle Channel between the Orkney and Shetland Isles. It was suggested that the highest priority should be given to the screening of catches of pelagic fish such as herring and mackerel obtained using gear fished close to the surface and in the areas through which post-smolts might be travelling.

Drs Hansen and Jacobsen, delegates from Norway, presented evidence that the marine distribution of Atlantic salmon was temperature dependent but whether distribution of food is an important factor was still an open question. It was pointed out that salmon leave the ocean feeding grounds after 1–4 years but the factors initiating homeward migration are unknown, but it is known that salmon have circannual rhythms of reproductive hormones, synchronised by photoperiod. The usual pattern is the older individuals return earlier in the season than the younger ones. However, the internal rhythms and responses to photoperiod are probably population specific. For example, salmon ascend several Scottish rivers in all months of the year, whereas in Norway and Iceland salmon ascend rivers only from May to October.

Little is known about the mechanisms of homing by salmon in the open ocean. It is suggested that the salmon may possess a compass orientation ability and head in a homeward direction without regard to their location at sea.

After salmon accomplish the migration from distant oceanic feeding grounds to the near shore environment, the coastal waters and estuaries present another set of challenges to their orientation systems. Salmon tracked by Smith off the east coast of Scotland showed their ability to swim in fixed directions at energetically efficient speeds but were also affected by tidal currents. The apparent random movements of many salmon in coastal waters and estuaries may not reflect orientation mechanisms but the tendency of many populations to wait for suitable conditions for upstream migration.

The juvenile salmon probably learn their way (imprint) sequentially during seaward migration and use that information when they return as adults.

Dr Bigg of the University of East Anglia in the conclusions to his talk on the historical and potential long-term climatic change in the North Atlantic pointed out that the North Atlantic is one of the most climatically sensitive regions of the world because of the interaction between oceanic and atmospheric processes that can occur. Atlantic salmon have had to adjust to large and temporally dramatic changes in ocean circulation and climate since the last glacial period. Such changes will continue in the near future, and may accelerate. He feels that if salmon are left to themselves they would probably adjust to the coming climate, but the challenge will be for our management of this resource to be as flexible as the salmon themselves.

In summary, it was agreed that there were a number of issues that required attention. It was considered essential that survival estimates for the whole life-cycle are obtained. In this regard, studies of growth patterns in historical scale collections could provide useful information. It was considered important to improve our understanding of the stage at which increased marine mortality occurs, and whether fish from different populations migrate to different areas of the North Atlantic where they are exposed to different conditions influencing their survival.

It was concluded from the literature relating growth, maturity and survival of salmon to climatic factors that the increased mortality of salmon in recent years may, in part, be climate-related. Evidence from research fishing in the northwest Atlantic indicates that salmon concentrate in waters in the temperature range 4–8°C and any change in ocean temperature could therefore lead to changes in distribution or to salmon experiencing sub-optimal conditions with possible effects on growth and survival.

Other factors that may affect survival are pollutants. For example, studies in New Brunswick suggested that 4-nonylphenol, a commercial compound widely used in industrial, commercial and domestic chemicals, including pesticides and cleaning products, may affect the later stages of smolting and lead to delayed mortality at sea. A number of organic contaminants enter the oceans and they include polychlorobiphenyls (PCBs), benzofurans, dioxins, aromatic hydrocarbons (PAHs) and organochlorines, a number of which may affect fish in different ways.

The proceedings of this workshop were published by Fishing News Books in 2000 under the title *The Ocean Life of Atlantic Salmon: Environmental and Biological Factors Influencing Survival.*

The enigma of the sea-life of salmon was gradually being solved and more results of marine investigations into the life of salmon in that environment were presented at the Sixth International Atlantic Salmon Symposium held in Edinburgh in 2002. Most of the presentations centred on further tracking of post-smolts in the Norwegian Sea and the Bay of Fundy and the deleterious effects of salmon farming.

Since the Second International Atlantic Salmon Symposium held in Edinburgh in 1978 salmon farms on the west coast of Scotland had been multiplying apace, as they had also in Norway and eastern Canada. The effects these farms were having on the local salmon and sea-trout populations had not been anticipated at the time the first farms were established but, as Ken Whelan had warned delegates at the 4th International Atlantic Salmon Symposium held in St. Andrews, Canada, there was growing evidence that sea lice infestation arising from the caged fish was affecting the survival of neighbouring sea-going smolts and returning adult fish. NASCO had convened meetings to discuss the growing problem of the effects of sea lice emanating from the caged fish had on wild fish and had published its findings.

Now, at the Sixth Atlantic Salmon Symposium, held in Edinburgh, delegates heard four alarming talks on this subject. These were: (i) Lice infection in Norwegian salmon stocks; (ii) Mortality of

*Sea lice on a salmon recently in from the sea. The number of sea lice present is about normal.
Had it been infested with sea lice from salmon farms it would have many more on its body.*

Atlantic salmon seaward migrating post-smolts – a salmon farmer's point of view; (iii) Finding a resolution to farmed salmon issues in North America, and (iv) Delivering the salmon - salmon sea lice infestation, sea lice production and sea-trout survival in Ireland, 1992–2001.

The situation with salmon farming and the fate of wild salmonids has still not been resolved.

CHAPTER SIX

The Future

It was becoming evident that catches of Atlantic salmon were declining and estimates of pre-fishery abundance also pointed in that direction. Anglers were gradually adopting a catch-and-release policy. In the United States the wild Atlantic salmon have been listed under the US endangered Species Act and in Canada some salmon populations have been listed under the Species at Risk Act.

As a result of declining catches of Atlantic salmon future research was now very much directed to its life at sea and an international programme of co-operative research called SALSEA was adopted in 2005. This was set up in response to concerns about the increased mortality of salmon at sea. NASCO established an International Salmon Research Board (IASRB) to promote collaboration and co-operation on research into the causes of marine mortality of Atlantic salmon and the opportunities to counteract this. By developing and reviewing an inventory of ongoing research the Board decided that its priority was studies on the migration and distribution of salmon at sea in relation to feeding opportunities and predation.

The SALSEA programme took advantage of recent advances in marine sampling, genetic techniques for stock identification, electronic tagging systems and scale analysis. These advances provided an opportunity to begin to unravel the secrets of the Atlantic salmon at sea and to shed new light on the causes of its decline.

The investigations relating to the distribution and migration of salmon at sea involved marine surveys in the Northeast (SALSEA Merge) and Northwest (SALSEA North America) Atlantic, and an enhanced programme of the internal-use fishery at West Greenland (SALSEA West Greenland). Additionally, the International Atlantic Salmon Research Board supported studies to re-examine historical tag recovery data from distant water fisheries and to investigate associations between changes in biological characteristics of Atlantic salmon, environmental changes and variations in marine survival. These investigations extended over approximately four or five years. The results were presented at a 'Salmon Summit' held at La Rochelle in 2011 and published in the ICES Journal of Marine Science (Vol. 69, Number 9) under the title *International Symposium on Salmon at Sea: Scientific Advances and their Implications for Management* (edited by Dr Peter Hutchinson).

With greatly reduced quotas for the Greenland salmon fishery, the present closure of the Faroese and Irish drift-net fisheries, the reduction in the Northumbrian drift-net fishery and the Scottish commercial salmon fisheries, and currently a catch and release policy for salmon anglers, it would be hoped that this might go some way to conserve salmon stocks. In 2017, owing to the new Scottish fisheries legislation passing through the Scottish Parliament, catch and release will become mandatory. All salmon nations in NASCO have strict laws regarding exploitation of their salmon stocks. This is all to the good but how are we to estimate the size of salmon populations in these countries? There are a number of methods that will help to provide data to estimate conservation limits that will be defined in the next paragraph. Fish traps are installed on some rivers, while rivers harnessed for power generation may have either counting facilities or electronic fish counters. In eastern Canada counting fences and trap nets to monitor the runs of adult salmon are operated by the Department of Fisheries and Oceans on the rivers Miramichi, Nepisiguit and Restigouche in New Brunswick; Sackville and Nashwaak in Nova Scotia, and on eleven rivers in Newfoundland and Labrador, including the Exploits, Cambelton and Terra Nova. On three eastern states in the United States of America there are counting facilities for migratory fish on the Penobscot and Connecticut Rivers. In Scotland there is a counter on the River North Esk operated by the Freshwater Fisheries Laboratory and fish counters are installed in the fish passes at a number of dams built for hydroelectric generation. These include Faskally on the Tummel at Pitlochry, Tor Achilty and Luichart on the Conon, Meig dam on the Meig, Aigas and Kilmorack on the Beauly and Lairg on the Shin. The Tweed Foundation had a fish counter on the Ettrick and one on the Gala Water, both tributaries of the Tweed. The Environment Agency monitor salmon numbers at their counters on the Tyne at Riding Mill, the Tees at the Tees Barrage, the Frome at East Stoke, the Leven in Cumbria and the Dee in Wales. There are numerous fish counters installed on Irish rivers, including on the Bush, the Faughan at Omagh, the Owengowla in Co. Galway and at Roe on the river Roe, all operated by the Loughs Agency. There is at least one river with a counter in Norway; the Målselva at Troms.

In addition to this information from rod catches and counters, data regarding salmon stocks is also obtained from electro-fishing surveys of juvenile salmon, supplemented in some areas with trapping of parr and smolts. NASCO recommends that juvenile surveys should be used to confirm the status of stocks and it is suggested that fisheries organisations work out their conservation limits. In other words their salmon stocks should be managed so that they have a high probability of exceeding a pre-defined minimum acceptable number – the Conservation Limit (CL). Conservation Limits have been set for most Irish salmon rivers and recreational and commercial inshore fisheries. These are now regulated relative to these conservation limits being met on a river-by-river basis

The conservation of salmon in England and Wales is the responsibility of the Environment Agency. In Scotland it falls between the Association of Scottish Salmon District Fishery Boards, fishery trusts and fishery foundations. However, things at present are in the melting pot as the Scottish government is reviewing the fisheries legislation with a view to changing the management arrangements and conservation policy including mandatory catch

The logos of the Atlantic Salmon Trust and the Atlantic Salmon Federation

and release. These proposals are included in the Wild Fisheries (Scotland) Bill that is out for consultation until May 2016.

While each country in NASCO has its own salmon laws the arrangement for the setting of quotas for Greenland and the Faroes has to be agreed by the Council of NASCO. Many other aspects of salmon conservation are also considered by NASCO including catch-and-release and salmon farming.

The Atlantic Salmon Trust and its North American counterpart the Atlantic Salmon Federation are, unfettered, able to pressurise government authorities when it comes to needing a deputation to put forward its reasons for objecting to a fishery policy that might endanger salmon stocks. The Trust also provides funds for research and it donated a significant sum of money to SALSEA. The Trust was one of the first NGOs when NASCO was established. The Medlar Press published a history of the Trust under the title *Salmon in Trust* in 2014.

The long-established Salmon and Trout Association, whose headquarters for many years was the Fishmongers' Company in London, would raise objections to any developments likely to affect salmon and trout stocks. More recently it assumed charitable status and changed its name to Salmon and Trout Conservation. At present it is running two campaigns, one to reduce or close salmon farms on the west coast of Scotland; the other is to attempt to persuade the Scottish government to close the coastal salmon netting stations that

The logos of Salmon & Trout Conservation UK and the North Atlantic Salmon Fund

are strictly speaking mixed stock fisheries, in other words they are harvesting fish in one area on the coast destined for many rivers.

France, too, has a similar organisation in the form of *L'Association Internationale de Défense du Saumons Atlantique.*

The North Atlantic Salmon Fund (NASF) that was established in 1989 was responsible for instigating the initial purchase of the Greenland quota and also the Faroese quota, the latter still being in force. Its aim to restore salmon stocks has been responsible for the buy-out or purchase of the Irish drift-net fishery and part funding of the purchase of the quotas of some of the fishermen engaged in the drift-net fishery off the Northumbrian and Yorkshire coast. Its energies are wide ranging through the work of its founder, Orri Vigfusson.

The river life of salmon is well managed and protected, but what is the future for its existence in the open ocean where man has no control over the environment? Some of the SALSEA projects will no doubt continue including genetic aspects involving studies that, for example, reveal that the features of a salmon scale can identify to which river a fish belonged.

There is some concern over the fate of post-smolts in their early months at sea when they might be 'harvested' by fishing vessels harvesting industrial species of fish such as herring, sprats and mackerel existing in the same areas as the post-smolts during their migrations to Faroese and Greenland waters. The Atlantic Salmon

The logo of the North Atlantic Salmon Conservation Organisation

Trust has had meetings with fishermen operating this fishery and some of the catches have also been inspected to determine whether or not any post-smolts have been found in the catches.

It is the vigilance of these Trusts that is so important and any action being taken by resource developers and harvesters that are liable to affect salmon survival do not go unchallenged.

Furthermore, many of these conservation trusts attend the Annual Meeting of the North Atlantic Salmon Conservation Organisation (NASCO) and are in a position to influence some of the decisions taken by this international gathering of salmon scientists and administrators.

Bibliography

Ashworth, Thomas. *The Salmon Fisheries of England*. Lewis, Bath, 1868.

Barbour, Andrew. *Atlantic Salmon: An Illustrated History*. Canongate Press, Edinburgh, 1992.

Bertram, James Glass. *The Harvest of the Sea; including sketches of fisheries and fisher folk*. Alexander Gardner, London & Paisley, 4th edition, 1885.

Brown, William. *The Natural History of the Salmon, as ascertained by the Recent Experiments in the Artificial Spawning and Hatching of the Ova and Rearing of the Fry, at Stormontfield on the Tay*. Thomas Murray, Glasgow, 1862.

Calderwood, William Leadbetter. *The Life of the Salmon, with reference more especially to the fish in Scotland*. Edward Arnold, London, 1907.

Calderwood, William Leadbetter. *Salmon and Sea Trout, with chapters on hydro-electric schemes, fish passes, etc*. Edward Arnold, London, 1930.

Calderwood, William Leadbetter. *Salmon Hatching and Salmon Migrations; Being the Buckland Lectures for 1930*. Edward Arnold, London, 1931.

Cushing, David Henry. *Climate and Fisheries*. Academic Press London, 1982.

Dahl, Knut. *The Age and Growth of Salmon and Trout in Norway, as shown by their scales*. The Salmon and Trout Association, London, 1916.

Flowerdew, Henry. *The Parr and Salmon Controversy*. Clark & Paterson, Edinburgh, 1871.

Friend, G F. *The Life History of the Salmon Gill-maggot, Salmincola salmonea (L) (Copepod crustacean)*. Transactions of the Royal Society of Edinburgh, 1942.

Hansen, Lars P; Hutchinson, Peter; Reddin, David G; & Windsor, Malcolm L. *International Symposium on Salmon at Sea: Scientific Advances and their Implications for Management*. ICES Journal for Marine Science. Vol. 69, Number 9, Oxford, 2012.

Hutton, James Arthur. *The Life History of the Salmon*. The University Press, Aberdeen, 1924.

Hutton, James Arthur. *Wye Salmon and Other Fish*. John Sherratt & Sons, Altrincham, 1949.

Johnston, H W. *The scales of the Tay salmon as indicative of age, growth and spawning habit*. 23rd Annual Report of the Fishery Board of Scotland, Appendix II, 1904.

Jones, John William. *The Salmon*. Collins New Naturalist Monograph, London, 1958.

Knox, Robert. *Fish and Fishing in the Lone Glens of Scotland – with a history of the propagation, growth and metamorphoses of the salmon*. G. Routledge, London, 1854.

Menzies, W J M. *The Salmon: It's Life Story*. William Blackwood, Edinburgh, 1925.

Menzies, W J M. *The Stock of Salmon: Its Migrations, Preservation and Improvement*. Being the Buckland Lectures for 1947. Edward Arnold, London, 1949.

Mills, Derek Henry. *The Ecology of the Young Stages of the Atlantic Salmon in the River Bran, Ross-shire*. Freshwater and Salmon Fisheries Research, No. 32, 1964.

Mills, Derek Henry. *Salmon and Trout: A Resource, its Ecology, Conservation and Management*. Oliver & Boyd, Edinburgh, 1971.

Mills, Derek Henry. *Scotland's King of Fish*. William Blackwood, Edinburgh, 1980.

Mills, Derek Henry. *Problems and Solutions in the Management of Open Seas Fisheries for Atlantic salmon*. The Atlantic Salmon Trust, Pitlochry, 1984.

Mills, Derek Henry. *Ecology and Management of Atlantic Salmon*. Chapman & Hall, London, 1989.

Mills, Derek Henry: Editor. *Tweed Towards 2000: A symposium on the future management of the Tweed fisheries*. The Tweed Foundation, Berwick-upon-Tweed, 1998.

Mills, Derek Henry: Editor. *Strategies for the Rehabilitation of Salmon Rivers*. Linnean Society, 1991.

Mills, Derek Henry: Editor. *Salmon in the Sea and New Enhancement Strategies*. (Proceedings of the Fourth International Atlantic Salmon Symposium held in St Andrews, New Brunswick, Canada, in June 1992). Fishing News Books, Oxford, 1993.

Mills, Derek Henry: Editor. *The Ocean Life of Atlantic Salmon: Environmental and Biological Factors Influencing its Survival*. Fishing News Books, Oxford, 2000.

Mills, Derek Henry. *Saving Scotland's Salmon*. Medlar Press, Ellesmere, 2009.

Mills, Derek Henry. *Salmon in Trust*. Medlar Press, Ellesmere, 2014

Mills, Derek & Graesser, Neil. *The Salmon Rivers of Scotland*. Cassell, London, 1981.

Mills, Derek & Noel Smart. *A Report on a Visit to the Faroes*. The Atlantic Salmon Trust, 1982.

Mills, Derek & David Piggins. *Atlantic Salmon: Planning for the Future*. Croom Helm, London, 1988.

Netboy, Anthony. *Atlantic Salmon: A Vanishing Species*. Faber and Faber, London, 1968.

Netboy, Anthony. *Salmon: The World's Most Harassed Fish*. Andrew Deutsch, London, 1980.

Paton, Diarmid Noel: Editor. *Report of Investigations on the Life-History of the Salmon in Fresh Water*. H.M.S.O., Fishery Board of Scotland: Salmon Fisheries, 1898.

Patterson, J H. *On The Cause of Salmon Disease: a bacterial investigation*. H.M.S.O., Fishery Board of Scotland, 1908.

Pentelow, F T K. *River Purification: a legal and scientific review of the last 100 years, being the Buckland Lectures for 1952*. Edward Arnold, London, 1953.

Pryce-Tannatt, Thomas Edwin. *Fish Passes: In connection with obstructions in salmon rivers, being the Buckland Lectures for 1937*. Edward Arnold, London, 1938.

Pyefinch, K A. *A Review of the Literature on the Biology of the Atlantic Salmon (Salmo salar)*. Freshwater and Salmon Fisheries Research, 9, 1955.

Pyefinch, K A & Mills, D H. *Observations on the Movements of Atlantic Salmon (Salmo salar L) in the River Conon and the River Meig, Ross-shire*. Freshwater and Salmon Fisheries Research, 31, 1963.

Scrope, William. *Days and Nights of Salmon Fishing in the River Tweed*. John Murray, Edinburgh, 1843.

Shearer, William Macdonald. *The Atlantic Salmon: Natural History, Exploitation and Future Management*. A Buckland Foundation Book, Fishing News Books, Oxford, 1992.

Shelton, Richard. *To Sea and Back: The Heroic Life of the Atlantic Salmon*. Atlantic Books, London, 2009.

Smith, Mordern W, & Carter, Wilfred M: Editors. *Proceedings of the International Atlantic Salmon Symposium: Management, Biology and Survival of the Species, 1972*. International Atlantic Salmon Foundation, St. Andrews, New Brunswick, Canada, 1973.

Sutterby, Rod & Greenhalgh, Malcolm. *Atlantic Salmon: An Illustrated Natural History*. Merlin Unwin Books, Ludlow, 2005.

Verspoor, Eric. *Genetics and Stocking in Tweed Towards 2000: A symposium on the future management of the Tweed fisheries*. Edited by Derek Mills. The Tweed Foundation, Berwick-upon-Tweed, 1998.

Went, Arthur Edward James. *Irish Salmon And Salmon Fisheries, being the Buckland Lectures for 1953*. Edward Arnold, London, 1955.

Went, Arthur Edward James: Editor. *Atlantic Salmon: Its Future*. The Proceedings of the Second International Atlantic Salmon Symposium, Edinburgh, 1978. Fishing News Books, Farnham, 1980.

Wigan, Michael. *The Salmon: The Extraordinary Story of the King of Fish*. William Collins, London, 2013.

Willughby, Francis & Ray, John. *De Historia Piscium*. The Royal Society, Oxford, 1686.

Youngson, Alan & Hay, David. *The Lives of Salmon: An illustrated account of the life-history of Atlantic salmon*. Swan Hill Press, Shrewsbury, 1996.